MAN, INTERRUPTED

Man, Interrupted

Welcome to the Bizarre World of OCD,
Where Once More is Never Enough

JAMES BAILEY

MAINSTREAM
PUBLISHING

EDINBURGH AND LONDON

First published in Great Britain in 2006 by
MAINSTREAM PUBLISHING COMPANY
(EDINBURGH) LTD
7 Albany Street
Edinburgh EH1 3UG

ISBN 1 84596 006 8

A catalogue record for this book is available
from the British Library

Typeset in Apollo and HeadlineTwo

Printed in Great Britain by
William Clowes Ltd, Beccles, Suffolk

FOREWORD

For those of us who take the simple things in life for granted – being able to flush a toilet *once* and carry on with our day, being able to eat without the paranoia that some germ in our food will kill us, washing our hands once and not thinking about it again – James Michael Bailey's book *Man, Interrupted* is a glance into what could happen if we suddenly got it all wrong and then, as part of our treatment, found ourselves having to confront all of the things that terrify us. With wit and humour, Bailey takes us into a world of insanity, rising to the occasion to heal himself, and along the way makes some very colourful friends.

Bailey is a patient with obsessive-compulsive disorder, and he hates and fears a lot of things: he is afraid of germs, of people who use drugs, of the idea of people putting hallucinogens in his food. He lives the depressing and tragic life of one afflicted by this mysterious condition. After years of living in his car and often battling suicidal notions, Bailey checks himself in to an institution full of people with the same complaints. He finds himself in a world of crazies, who are all, like him, struggling to overcome their 'disease' and get well. However, Bailey's stay at the hospital is more often than not humorous, as it includes him spending most of his recovery time hitting on younger, Asian women (an obvious obsession of his) and then, when he tries to hang out with druggies in

Berkeley to cure him of his fears, being regarded as a 'nark' for never joining in with their drug-taking.

Having lived and worked in Hollywood for almost 25 years, I have a theory that *all* of us are walking a tightrope as far as our own sanity is concerned. This book hilariously confirms that yes, we might all have the potential for that slip into insanity, but we all have the power of the human spirit to overcome even our worst nightmares. As I have got to know Bailey, I have found a warm, comforting friend and someone whom I respect, not least for his own ability to overcome the chemical, mental or whatever imbalance that life imposed on him and to deal with the situation with humour, passion and heart.

This is a must-read book for everyone. I promise that no sunrise, no cup of coffee and no shared moment with a loved one will ever be the same.

I have been in the film business for 23 years, having started as an agent trainee at the William Morris Agency. Subsequently I worked for producer Lawrence Turman of the Turman-Foster Company at MGM, then went on to be a freelance reader at United Artists and Triad Artists. Then I had the dream job as an executive at Steven Spielberg's Amblin Entertainment for close to five years, which was a truly magical experience. After leaving Amblin, I became a literary agent at BBMW and then in 1990 started my own company, Viviano Entertainment, as a literary manager and film and television producer. Since then I have partnered with ex-ICM agent Richard Feldman, and our company, Viviano-Feldman Entertainment, is located in Beverly Hills, California.

Bettina Sofia Viviano

PROLOGUE

Sweat began to drip down my forehead and onto my fingers. Louisiana humidity had nothing to do with it this time. This was a defining moment to find out what I was made of, and what I had become.

The gun pointing at my temple could easily go off now without much effort.

It all seemed surreal as some heavy-metal band blasted away on the radio. My obituary would say something like, 'A sad life came to a sad end in the parking lot of a burger bar.'

The music became louder and louder. I hadn't touched the knob.

Anxiety kicked in, more intense than I could bear.

The faceless waitress who had served me that lunchtime was tormenting my brain. Her voice kept running through my head. But not her face; never the face: a face can tell too many lies.

We'd chatted as she'd served me my burger and fries. I'd told her I was obsessive about my health and she'd said with a grin, 'Why would you eat hamburgers if you're such a health nut? There has to be all kinds of bad chemicals in a burger!'

Hours after I'd eaten my meal, her words had suddenly leapt back into my head. Why had she said 'bad chemicals'? Did that mean she'd put something in my burger? Some remote part of me knew she hadn't. The other part, the part with 'delusions and what ifs', needed her to reassure me. I'd driven back to the restaurant, planning to go in and ask her, but I didn't have the strength or the will to go through with it. I had asked enough times in my life.

My fingers began to slide. Maybe my psyche had had enough. Years of pain and suffering with obsessive-compulsive disorder (OCD) had burnt me out. It was time to end the continuous questions that flooded my brain – questions and concerns that I knew the answers to, but couldn't convince myself to believe. Had I lost trust even in myself? The only conclusion I could find became clear: I came into the world alone and I would die alone.

My body began to shake as I prepared for the end.

Yes, do the world a favour!

Yet there was some slight hesitation, although I had no idea why: what the fuck did I have to live for?

A moment later the waitress walked out of the restaurant and approached her car. Was it a sign? I put the gun down slowly and ran over to her.

She would give me some kind of reassurance and I would be OK. She would think I was a freak, but that wouldn't matter. I needed this reaction to see that my fears were irrational: there was nothing in the burger and I wasn't going to get high. My anxiety would go back to manageable levels again and I'd get on with my life – at least, until the next time a random stranger inadvertently pressed my panic button and drove me back to the brink of suicide.

That's just the way I was back then.

MAN, INTERRUPTED

TRIUMPH

When did my problems really begin? I have thought about that question for years and years. I guess my first anxiety attack came when I was five. Of course, back then they didn't call it that.

At that time my father and mother had just got a divorce in Kansas and the court awarded custody of me, my brother and sister to my mother. That would have been great, but unfortunately my mother said she wasn't getting enough child support for all of us and kept only my sister. I still vividly remember them dragging me out of her car as I clung to the seat. I stared at my sister as they drove away towards Minnesota, my mom's home state.

A couple of years later, living with my dad and Step-Mom Number One, I ended up being taken to the emergency room for some imaginary pain in my back. In retrospect, that was the beginning of the end that led me here.

Why couldn't it have been me instead of my sister? The vision of them driving away haunts me even to this day. Why did it affect me and not my brother? He's led a perfectly normal life and is married with kids and a dog. I later got back with my mother when I was 13, but the damage was done. My mind was always working. I couldn't stop it. What was wrong with me? Why had I been rejected?

It's weird that I'd even made it this far. Here I was, in 2000, a full-blown OCD sufferer for the last 25 years, sitting on my butt wondering if I really had the nerve to come to Berkeley and the esteemed Triumph Psychiatric Hospital.

I should thank God and Evon for my discovering Triumph. Evon was a girl I'd met about a year before, jogging on Town Lake in Austin, Texas. In actuality, I don't know why I was in Austin at all. I do know I was living out of a truck and, for some bizarre reason unknown to me, that suited me just fine.

If you've been to Austin, you would say Town Lake is the nicest place in the world to jog. It has this great trail that goes around this beautiful clear lake in the hill country of Texas. Of course, adding to the natural beauty are scores of sexy women there day and night.

Evon was a sweet girl who was impressed with my running both mornings and evenings. She didn't know that I was deliberately obsessing about it to avoid the severe anxiety attacks and depression that came from obsessing about other things. She just assumed I was a health nut, and that was fine by me. We ended up having a nice chat and when she was leaving she said, 'Email me so we can keep in touch.'

The dreaded email again. I had been meeting girls for several years and it always ended up with, 'Email me some time.'

I'm sure Evon, like most of the other gals I had met, was afraid I was about to ask for her telephone number. Of course, this was a safety measure. If someone acts weird in an email it's easy to block any further correspondence. I didn't take it personally because I knew most guys were getting similar treatment.

Problem was I was computer illiterate. I had a double whammy. Not only was I intimidated by the Net, I also had no access to it. That all changed when Evon said, 'Meet me at the public library tomorrow and in ten minutes I'll get you a Yahoo address and you're off and running.'

I met Evon that next morning and she was basically right. I must say I am very slow to catch onto things, but once I do . . .

I found out quickly that the Net was used for far more

than just exchanging emails. I don't remember the exact thought that precipitated it — I'm sure it was sheer desperation, as I'd had enough of living in total terror — but I soon found myself checking for hospitals that specialised in obsessive-compulsive disorders.

There were several listed, and UCLA was my first choice because I was familiar with LA, having lived there before. Unfortunately, they only had an outpatient clinic and I needed someplace where I could stay in-house. I ended up finding 'Within Reach', a house connected to Triumph Psychiatric Hospital in Berkeley, California.

I emailed them and had my local psychiatrist forward the necessary paperwork. I got onto the long waiting list and ended up moving back to Louisiana. A year of on-and-off suicidal periods later, my residential invitation arrived in the post. I nearly lost my nerve a few days before the crunch time arrived and tried to talk myself out of it, telling myself I was getting better. Deep down, though, I knew this was my last chance, so I found the courage to follow it through.

Even though I never saw Evon again, she was inadvertently responsible for me being alive today.

THE ARRIVAL

The taxi pulled up in front of the sign that read Triumph Psychiatric Hospital. It suddenly began to rain. Was that an omen?

It dawned on me why you always see a cab pulling up in front of a hospital in those movies about people with emotional problems. The director is symbolising that this is just the beginning of the journey, not the end.

The cab drove up to Within Reach, the house behind

Triumph where I would be staying. Somehow, it had looked better in the brochure they'd sent me. Hell, I'd had to wait almost a year to get in. I guess after suffering for 25 years, what's another year, right?

The cabbie got out and pulled my suitcase out of the trunk. He looked like a cabbie: the look of a guy who never slept and whose diet consisted of endless cups of coffee and unfiltered cigarettes, and whose idea of healthy eating was an occasional fish sandwich at McDonald's.

I got out and was debating what kind of tip I should give him, since I'd already given him the fare in advance at the airport. As I turned to look at him, he darted into his cab and drove off. I knew what he was thinking. He was afraid I was a wacko and feared I might do something to him. No wonder he hadn't said a word all the way here. I would be thinking about this way into the night. What can I say? This is the life of a guy with OCD.

I grabbed my luggage and opened the front door.

'Are you James, the new patient?'

A tall, skinny guy said this to me as he blocked my path. I nodded.

'James, you are not allowed to use this door. It's only for staff.'

He told me to go back around to the front of the house.

Of course, that was not the greeting I was expecting, but at least it took my mind off the cabbie. I stumbled around to the front, looking for the entrance, when I was pleasantly surprised by this cute blonde who popped out of nowhere.

'You must be James Bailey. We've been expecting you. Take your luggage and follow me to your room.'

I grabbed my luggage and walked in, but somehow the blonde had disappeared. I looked around until I spotted blondie talking to the dude who'd given me that great welcoming party. Before I was able to yell out to her, though, she ran off into another room.

I figured this was a good time to use the bathroom, since I'd been holding it in during the cab ride. I walked up to a guy with a crew cut who was standing behind one of those doors with its bottom half closed and its top half open so the patients don't actually get inside the office. I asked him where the toilets were.

'Number one or number two?' he asked.

'What I mainly want is a dump.'

'We don't talk that way around here, James. It's number one or number two.'

This guy must have been expecting me too. I knew he was going to be a problem.

'Well, sir, when I go to do number two, I usually have a little number one going on, too. So what would that be?'

He hesitated for a moment. I knew exactly what he was thinking: I can't let this patient get to me; I'm the educated professional here. He handed me a key and a small roll of toilet paper with just a few sheets on it and started to shut the top half of the door. I stuck my hand in to prevent him from closing it.

'Hey, buddy, I'll need a little more than that!'

He gave me a funny look.

'That's how we cure your OCD.'

'I don't have a problem with toilet paper!'

He told me that I'd have to wait till later, when he'd had a chance to check the files, and if that really wasn't a problem of mine, I would be allowed to take a proper roll in with me. I started mouthing off and, before I could finish, the cubicle was shut. Now I was getting upset. The cute blonde walked up.

'I heard you say you have to use the bathroom.'

'I did, but now, after all this, I've lost that feeling.'

'Then you won't be needing this.'

She grabbed the key and the miniature toilet roll from my hands.

'Why did you do that?' I said.

'We can't have you hoarding toilet paper.'

'Listen, a mosquito couldn't wipe his butt with that!'

I guess I wasn't surprised when she didn't respond. I couldn't say I blamed her. A moment later, she spoke.

'You ready to go to your room?'

'Sure.'

I followed the little blonde up the staircase as she told me her name was Mary and that the guy with the crew cut was Harry.

'I think that guy has an attitude,' I said to her.

She didn't respond. She showed me my room.

'Oh, James, the maid must have forgotten to clean and sanitise the mattress.'

I looked on, a little shell shocked. The mattress was one of those prison types: hard as rock, with a big slit in it. Plus, you don't mention the word 'sanitise' around a person with OCD! Our brains all kick in with, 'Why does it need sanitising?'

'I will just take that bed over there, Sherry.'

I pointed to an already made-up bed on the other side of the room.

'My name is Mary and, no, that bed is for Raymond, your roommate.'

'Who slept on it before, miss, and why does it need sanitising?' I said.

'You're asking for reassurance, James, and we don't allow that here. Be it from staff or fellow patients.'

'Thanks, Mary, because now I'm having a full-blown anxiety attack!'

'Don't worry, James, I'll go ask Harry what to do.'

'Was the last patient a drug addict? Is that why there's a slit in the mattress?'

'Reassurance again, James.'

I tried not to ask her again, but the anxiety running through me was too much to ignore.

'Come on, you're the one who started it with that "it needs sanitising" remark.'

Mary just stared at me. I didn't know at the time that deliberately worrying remarks such as this were part of the treatment, and it had sent my panic into overdrive.

'Yes, I need fricking reassurance!'

Mary just shook her head and ran down the stairs.

It dawned on me that the only way I was going to get reassurance around this place was to check the bed myself. It also dawned on me that I was causing a big commotion and I'd only arrived a few minutes earlier. I'd been on the waiting list for over a year, so why had I made an entrance like that? I quickly put it down to 'self-sabotage', but more about that later. My mind was on the mattress.

I slowly made my way to the bed, making sure I wasn't getting too close. I tried to imagine some positive reason why there would be a slit in the mattress. Maybe the guy had been hiding soap in the mattress because he had such a fear of germs. Maybe he'd farted so hard he'd blown holes in it. Maybe he'd made the slits to hide his porno magazines. Of course, he'd been depressed, but he was totally against drugs, right?

I knew I was in the middle of an obsession and my compulsion – getting reassurance – was not going to be sated by Mary. I also knew I had to do something before it turned into a full-blown anxiety attack! I looked to the other side of the room and tried to focus on my roommate's well-made bed. They'd told me in the email I would be living with twenty others like myself. Twenty other freaks, I'd thought to myself. That had scared the hell out of me. I couldn't even be in the same room with one person for longer than ten minutes without having an anxiety attack.

Just then, Mary re-entered the room. 'Harry says you can change rooms. You get to have two roommates now. Isn't that great?'

On cue, a highly camp-sounding guy yelled out from the next room. 'Hi, I'm Adam. You can be our roommate!'

Oh, Lord. Now, I had nothing against gays, but I didn't want to room with one either.

'Listen, can't we just change mattresses, miss?'

She hesitated for a moment, then said, 'Let me go ask Harry.'

I sat around on the floor for what seemed like a half-hour, waiting for the girl. It finally dawned on me that she wasn't coming back. During her absence I wondered why I was such a homophobe. I soon remembered an issue I used to keep thinking about many moons ago: maybe I was gay. Finally I got up and walked downstairs.

As I was about to hit the last step, a big fat guy popped out of nowhere and stuck out his hand.

'I'm Tim. Glad to meet you.'

I didn't want to shake his hand, but it was too late. His big paw engulfed my hand. I now needed to go and wash it, but how? Harry had the only key to the bathroom. I looked up at the fat guy. He was sweating like a pig and his face was covered with zits. Oh, man, my hand and fingers had to be crawling with germs now! What if he'd just taken a number two and wiped his big butt with that little sheet of paper?

Oh, God, I had to get in the bathroom and fast. I ran over to the cubicle and knocked on the door.

Harry answered.

'Uh, Harry, can I change the mattress and I, uh, got to get the key to the restroom?'

'Another patient has the key so you'll have to wait and I already changed the mattress.'

The door was quickly closed. How in the hell did he change the mattress? He couldn't have got by me – there was only one way and I would have seen him. I ran after Mary again and said, 'How did he change the mattress? I just came down the stairway and there is no way he could have gotten by me! I am going back upstairs and dragging that mattress down here and daring him to close that door on me!'

I ran upstairs. I looked in my room and there was the same mattress. I was having a full-frontal anxiety attack and had to act quickly. I ran into the next room to change the mattress myself. There, sitting on the only unmade bed, was a mattress with the exact same slit as mine. Were they doing this on purpose just to test me, or was I imagining both of the slits?

Just then I heard a loud voice coming from the hallway. I ran out and this hot-looking brunette, whom I would later find out was a counsellor named Dorwina, was yelling to someone in the bathroom to get out.

'Get out, Barney! You have washed far past your ten-minute limit.'

I walked by her and said, 'Do you know, I've been so busy trying to change my mattress, I don't feel the need to wash my hands any more.'

'OCD?' she said to me.

'Yeah, OCD.'

When I went back to my room that evening, exhausted, I

was surprised to find my bed neatly made up. I lay down and found the mattress to be very comfortable. I guess the slit in it was pretty tiny after all, and I'd really made a fuss about nothing. The guy in the bed next to me didn't say much before I dropped off, and I was glad. All I remember him saying was that he was from Philly.

MORNING

I awoke to the sound of loud voices yelling for us all to get up. I slowly made my way downstairs. The drugs I was on made it hell to wake up in the morning. I'd started taking antidepressants and some anti-psychotic medicine about a month before arriving here. I'd been terrified of them at first. My OCD applied to all drugs – prescription as well as 'leisure' – but it had been a simple choice: either I took them, or I'd end up killing myself. I'd had time to mentally adjust to taking them now, but I still wasn't sure what effect they were having. All I really knew about the anti-psychotic one was that it put about 20 lb on me. I guess the good news about it was that, when taking it, I had no trouble sleeping.

I saw a bunch of people lined up as I walked into the living room. I figured it was the queue for breakfast, so I jumped in. A few moments later an older woman yelled out, 'Morning meds! Anyone for meds, get in line!'

Now I started feeling a little better. I only took meds at night, so at least I wasn't as drugged up as everyone else. I worked my way to the kitchen. The older woman walked by and told me to help myself to cereal, coffee, fruits and all kinds of other things. I hadn't eaten those types of foods in a long time. I was visibly excited. I filled a bowl and was just about to tuck into its contents when I heard this loud voice say, 'Meeting time! Right now or you get written down as late. Barney, you are getting written up again and don't tell me you didn't know that we don't allow food in here.'

Oh, boy, I was starving, but I didn't want to be written up on my first day. I walked in and sat down. I looked around the room. There were about 20 people there. I was trying to figure out where they all came from. I noticed three really good-looking girls sitting together. Most of the guys looked like losers, but, then again, they were probably thinking the same thing about me.

The three attractive girls started speaking. Guess what? They were all counsellors. I started thinking that Dr Swenson, the famous psychiatrist from Sweden who ran the place, must be a womaniser to have hired all these young girls. If that was the case, then maybe we would hit it off.

Just then, the cute blonde who had showed me to my room stood up.

'James, I'm Mary and we'd all like to welcome you to Within Reach.'

The other two said hello and gave their names, but I was only interested in Mary. Because of my anxiety when I'd first arrived, I hadn't realised how hot she was. When a guy who was obviously a patient got up and started to explain the programme, I blurted out, 'I want you to explain it, Mary. Not this clown!'

Dorwina, the woman from the hallway, stood up and said, 'Barney is trying to help you, so please don't be rude to him.'

'Hey, Dorpina, it's not my fault the guy looks like a geek!'

MY BEHAVIOUR THERAPIST

The next thing I knew I'd been whisked out to another building and was sitting behind the desk of this tall, skinny woman who looked like Olive Oyl. I snapped out of my disorientated daydreaming when she spoke.

'Well, James, I'm Tonya, your behaviour therapist. I'll be the one who will guide you to your exposures, and will be the one to decide the best programmes for you. First of all, though, you were rude to Harry and told Mary you didn't like Harry. You were also rude to Barney and Dorwina.'

'It's not my fault the guy looks like Mr Bean.'

Tonya looked on like, enough already!

'Am I in big trouble?' I sheepishly said.

'No, but you need to remember you came a long way from Louisiana to get better, right?'

She was right. Within a few hours of my arrival I'd managed to insult a fellow patient and two or three counsellors. I always seemed to sabotage myself in everything.

'OK, James, let's get serious. Tomorrow you will go down to Telegraph Avenue and People's Park to work on exposures.'

'What are exposures?'

'I'll get to that later. Now, I know about your drug thing from reading the notes. Is there anything else I should know?'

'I just started with the hand washing about a year ago. I mean, shaking hands or anything I touch contaminates me and then I contaminate anything I touch. I even ruined my electric car windows. I shorted out the wires washing them and almost electrocuted myself!'

Tonya burst out laughing.

'Hey, Tonya, it's not that funny.'

'I'm sorry, James. I wasn't laughing at you. It's the situation.'

'OK, Tonya, it does seem kind of funny now. I mean, not too many people try to clean hot electrical wires with soap and water. I couldn't tell you how many remote controls I've screwed up. You ever heard of anyone washing their remote controls with soap and water? How about turning faucets off with their feet? Or washing their money with shampoo? Every time I go get groceries I give the cashiers wet and soapy bills. You should see all the cashiers running for cover when they see me pull up! My OCD has gotten so bad that homeless people wait outside the grocery store for me because they know, two out of three times, I'll throw the whole fricking bag of groceries out the window. Why, you ask? Because I notice something that doesn't look just right, on the receipt, or the label, etc. Hell, one of those drunken bastards even had the nerve to come up to me one day and say, "Hey, if you're going to throw 'em out today, can you do it now, 'cause I'm too hung over to follow you down the street." I could have killed that bastard! I mean, you talk about gall.'

Tonya and I both laughed at what I said.

'Then I have this word thing. If anyone says "high" or "freak" or "trip", like in a conversation, well, I immediately have a panic attack like somehow they're insinuating I'm high or getting high and so on. To make the anxiety go away, I have to say things like, "You didn't mean I was high, did you?" and so on. Most of the time I know they're just using slang terms but I still need some kind of reassurance.'

'You obsess about what somebody says in a conversation and in order to get rid of the obsession you do your ritual, ask for reassurance,' said Tonya.

'You got it,' I said.

I could have gone on and on for hours about my bizarre lifestyle but decided to do us both a favour and change the subject. 'What's the deal with Telegraph Avenue and People's Park?' I asked.

'Telegraph Avenue has the main Berkeley campus at one end of it, so it's a university area: cafés, coffee shops, bookstores, etc. People's Park is just off it. It's full of street people: the druggies, the freaks, the runaways . . .'

'Druggies and freaks!' I said.

'James, I'm not going to give you any reassurance.'

'You just said freaks to see how I'd react, right?'

'I'm not going to respond to that, James. Tomorrow you'll go down there for about 45 minutes and hang out. I want you to shake hands and mingle.'

'Shake hands?' I said.

'Yes, shake hands and fight that immediate urge to go and wash. We call these exposures. The longer you hang in there, the better. Your anxiety will decrease the longer you expose yourself to your irrational fears. After a while, you'll get desensitised.'

Boy, the thought of hanging out with a bunch of freaks scared the hell out of me. I had been avoiding freaks for 25 years and now she wanted me to sit, hang and even touch them. Just the word drove me crazy. You know what was ironic? I'm the freak.

Tonya asked me what my mind was drifting about. I panicked.

'Drifting? What do you mean by drifting?'

She got angry.

'You know what I'm talking about.'

I felt calmer. When somebody gets mad at me for asking for reassurance, it usually calms me down.

'There's something else I want to tell you. I met this girl once in Denver at a supermarket, and she invited me over to her house. After a while I started acting a little hyper and weird, so she asked me to leave. Right before I left, she said she hoped I wasn't crazy and wasn't going to trip out and do something. After I got home, I started thinking about what she'd said. I was thinking that maybe she'd put drugs or something in the popcorn we ate, and that's what she meant by tripping out. Part of me knew that that wasn't rational thinking. But the next day, my anxiety was so intense it was either get reassurance from her or kill myself!'

Tonya had a bewildered look on her face. She must have heard some doozies over the years but, right now, I had her full attention.

'I went over to her apartment building and hid behind some cars and waited all day for her to show up. I'll never forget the look on her face when she spotted me in front of her building.'

'What did you say?'

'I made up the story I used hundreds of times. I said someone had put something in my best friend's food years ago and he died, and I was afraid that someone would do it to me. Then I asked her if she put anything in the popcorn.'

'What happened next?' said Tonya.

'The girl looked at me like I was crazy and told me of course not. Then I started asking her what she meant by "not". I asked her ten times if she said did or did not. I'm sure she was scared, and that's the only reason she kept appeasing me. Finally, the anxiety wilted. I told her thanks and that I would never bother her again. I'm sure she went into her apartment and promised herself never to talk to strangers again.'

'I'm surprised you've never been arrested or beaten up. Or have you?' said Tonya.

'Luckily, I've never been arrested and as far as me being beaten up, I've been beaten up my whole life in one way or another. You can't hurt me physically. My self-justification was easy, too. Either I asked for reassurance or I committed suicide. So they're a little frightened and inconvenienced for a while. For me it's life and death, and getting reassurance enables me to live on, until the next encounter.'

'Yes, James, but think about this: people, I mean complete strangers, have all that power over you. Doesn't that piss you off?'

I had to take a step back and digest this. She was right. That really did piss me off. Any schmuck off the street could overpower me with just one little word. I told her I'd even driven back 70 miles out of my way once because I'd remembered a word a cashier said at a seven–eleven that sparked my need for reassurance. Tonya said I should use that anger as a motivational tool. But she added that it sounded more like paranoia. I told her I had thought so too, and that I'd told Dr Swenson some of these things on my original questionnaire and he'd said, 'Don't worry. Just come on in. We can help you.'

'Just remember, James,' responded Tonya, 'the longer you hang in there tomorrow, the better. Believe it or not, the anxiety will eventually go away. Just keep reminding yourself every time you want to go and wash your hands that there are goals in life that you want to attain, and that this illness is preventing you from having a happy and productive life. Other people have beaten it with hard work and determination. Why not you? Every time you feel the strong need to wash or ask for reassurance just keep telling yourself that. If necessary, take it minute by minute. Like you're in a race and the prize is a happy and fulfilling life.'

'Tonya, I was weird even before the OCD kicked in. I ran away from Kansas when I was just seven years old.'

'Ran away from home, James?'

'No, Tonya. You don't run away if you have a home. It would be more accurate to say I ran away from where I was staying. And I was staying with my dad and Step-Mom Number One at the time.'

I got Tonya's full attention. She was waiting for my next words. I couldn't decide if I wanted to go any further. Maybe I'd opened a can of worms that I wouldn't be able to deal with.

'Where did you go?' said Tonya.

'I got on the highway and started hitchhiking towards Minnesota. I kept thinking someone I knew was going to stop and take me home.'

Tonya's eyes were fully focused. 'Did you find that someone, James?'

'No. It was just a fantasy. There was no home for me.'

There was dead silence. Why was I opening up to this woman? I trusted no one. Maybe I was trying to tell her why I had a chip on my shoulder, and thus explain my rude behaviour to everyone that morning. I could sense I was choking up and had to go in another direction.

'It's OK to cry, James.'

'Me, cry? I got something in my eye. I don't cry, Tonya.'

I had to go in another direction and fast!

'You know, Tonya, when you're weird in Louisiana and Kansas and Minnesota, well, that's one thing. But if you move to, say, LA and you're still considered weird . . . well, you get the picture.'

I had succeeded in changing the subject.

Of course, Tonya told me that being weird was just being unique. I liked the way she said unique. That would be another mantra for me. 'No, I am not weird. I am unique!'

Tonya told me that would be all for the day and that we would meet three times a week. As I got up to leave, I said something I would deeply regret.

'How's the weather up there, Olive Oyl?'

She stared at me for a moment before speaking. 'You think because I'm tall I can't be a good therapist?'

Why did I say that? I've asked myself that a million times. I always had to open my big fricking mouth.

I finally spoke. 'I know the brochure said we usually stay about two or three months, but who actually decides the exact time?'

'I do. Have a nice day, James.'

I walked out of her office angry with myself.

I ran into the big fat guy again as I made my way back to the house. This time, without hesitation, I stuck my hand out to shake his.

'Don't touch my hands! I don't like to shake hands,' he said.

Now I was really confused. Wasn't he the one who stuck his big sweaty hand out and grabbed mine just yesterday? He turned and walked away. I started thinking crazy again. What was on his hands? Drugs or something? I walked down the steps trying to get a grip on my now rising anxiety when I heard the fat guy call my name. I turned around.

'Who's your BT?' he asked.

'Tonya,' I said.

'Don't say anything about her height. She's very sensitive about that.'

DINNER

Dinner with 20 people was going to be a trip! It's funny, if I said that word to myself, it didn't bother me, but if someone else said it – well, you know the story. I can have a conversation with someone and hours later my mind will detect any little word, or even the slightest hint of one, that suggests being high.

One day this cute girl I met on the beach asked me how my jog was. I just went nuts! I asked her what she meant: why wouldn't I have a good jog, and had she done something to me to keep me from having a good jog? The girl took off like a scalded dog. And this was a pretty typical occurrence. I wouldn't have given it a second thought if the girl wasn't so cute.

The food was the best thing about Within Reach so far. There was beef and potatoes and salads. I hadn't seen food like that in years. As I began to fill my plate, though, a thought came back to me like a bolt of lightning: all these other patients were on some kind of drugs, and most were on something much stronger than what I was taking. I could just about cope with my own drugs, but other people's . . .? How could I touch the forks and glasses and pitchers of water and ice tea that everyone else was touching without going crazy?

Surprisingly, a wave of confidence hit me. My medication must have kicked in because I felt no anxiety. I surveyed the table as I ate. I figured I would keep a low profile and see how the wind blew around here. The staff more or less ate together with us. I'd never seen so many cute girls all in one group before. Mary was my favourite, even though I'd pissed her off when I first arrived.

I surveyed the rest of the patients. The gals all looked

pretty rough, except one. I found out later her name was Anna. She was very attractive and talked a mile a minute. Everybody listened as she went off on a panicked monologue about Aids. Even here, beauty took top billing. If I or any other patient was doing this, everyone would be annoyed. She had everybody grasping for the next words out of her mouth for one reason: she was HOT!

She was also the definition of the word 'wired'. She went on and on about her fear of Aids. This put me off her soon enough and I tried not to listen to her, although I wondered what her exposure was going to be. Anna finally got off the Aids and started in about how she had such a great boyfriend and how he was coming to visit her the next night. I later found out that we could have visitors downstairs from 7 to 9 p.m.

I suddenly noticed the big fat guy wasn't at the table. I knew his fear couldn't be of food, so where was he?

After dinner, we went to the main room for our last group. They had split us up and I was thrilled when the Aids girl was in the other group. My luck was getting even better when I found out that Mary was the counsellor for my group.

As Mary began to speak, the big fat guy came barrelling in. They told him he was five minutes late and that he wasn't allowed to enter the group. He had to be written up. I'd been there a very short time and had seen three people written up already!

Mary started the group and explained to me how it worked. 'What we do during exposure, James, is to try and get our anxiety level as high as we can stand it. For instance, if your OCD was a fear of touching doorknobs because of germ contamination, then you would place your hands on the knob as long as possible before giving in to your compulsion of washing them. You rate your anxiety before, during and after you finish your exposure. The exposure works by desensitising you little by little. In other words, you go towards your fears, instead of away from them. The power they have over you will get less and less.'

She told us to rate our anxiety levels each day from one to ten, with ten being the highest. She started to go to another subject when Barney blurted out, 'Hey, Mary, you forgot to tell him to set a goal every day regarding his OCD.'

'Yes, James, I was just going to add that.'

'You never said thanks for correcting you, Mary,' said Barney.

Mary was getting visibly annoyed with Barney but kept her cool, somehow. 'Thank you, Barney,' said Mary.

'Hey, where am I going for exposure?' said Barney. Mary just bit her lip and ignored him.

'My goal is to get better,' I said.

'You have to be more specific,' said Barney.

Mary's face turned bright red. She was beside herself.

'He wasn't specific enough, Mary!'

I watched Barney and Mary go back and forth. It was good because all the attention was off me. At least for now. Barney was relentless. He looked like this guy in one of my sixth-grade schools. I say one because I went to three or four sixth-grade schools, all in different towns, as my relatives were scattered around and I was shipped between them. I even repeated sixth grade because I met these nice guys playing baseball who were all going into the sixth grade, even though I had passed to seventh in some other town in some other state. I'd asked the people I was staying with at the time if it was OK if I took sixth grade over again. Of course, they said sure, without blinking an eye.

Barney looked like this schoolkid named Robert 'Little

Mouth'. He had the same pointed nose, skinny face and small mouth.

'James, would you mind waking up and telling us your specific goal for today?' Mary's voice brought me out of my daydream.

'Well, Mary, I won't ask reassurance from anybody at Telegraph Avenue.'

'Ask reassurance about what?' said Barney.

To be honest I didn't blame the guy. He was getting me back for calling him a geek in front of Mary that morning. My mind froze. I didn't know what to say. I found myself staring across the room, looking for some kind of quick inspiration. I noticed this one pretty girl fiddling with her hands. They looked like the hands of an old woman, even though she couldn't have been over 30.

I met this famous actress once in LA who had to be around 60. She must have had plastic surgery because her face looked great. The hands, though – she had those hands only old people get. Once I saw that, I knew she had to be old. But she was a very nice lady.

'James, reassurance about . . . .?' repeated Barney.

I felt cornered. I certainly didn't trust anybody here to tell them my weaknesses. I mean, guys like Barney would have had a field day with this. I didn't tell Barney to mind his own damn business, which would have been the norm for me. Instead, I responded calmly. 'My BT told me not to disclose anything about my problems yet.'

Barney wasn't letting me off that easily. 'None of us at Within Reach are afraid to share our problems, James.'

I was starting to get anxious when the pretty girl with the chapped hands came to the rescue. 'James doesn't have to explain anything to any of us unless he wants to, Barney.'

'That's right, Lisa,' said Mary.

I fell in love with Lisa at that moment. Well, I should say, as much in love as I'm capable of, but that's another story.

'I try and help the guy and he pops off,' said Barney.

I knew then that Barney wasn't going to let go. I had embarrassed him in front of Mary, and, of course, he and every male here had a crush on her. Hell, I had a crush on her, too, and I had only been here for one night. Of course, Mary was way beyond any of us; even in my anxiety-ridden condition, I was aware of that.

'Barney, enough already. Tell us your plan for today, Barney,' said Mary.

'I will not do this more than three times today.'

'Do what?' said Mary.

'This!' Barney lifted up his legs and cut a big fart! Everybody broke out in laughter, even Mary. Barney quickly added, 'Hey, you can't write me up for that because when it wants to come out, it has to come out!'

I think Barney must have got scared because, after the laughter died down, he got unusually quiet.

Every patient did his or her little spiel and then Mary asked us if anybody had anything to say. A girl got up and said the staff had told her that this was to be her last week here. But her day was a one and her anxiety was a nine.

'Miss, it seems to me that if you're leaving this week, your day should be a nine or a ten and your anxiety a one or a two,' I said.

She didn't respond.

Just then Lisa blurted out, 'Give me the keys to the bathroom because I touched the bottom of the chair and it's crawling with germs!'

Mary told her no. Group was in session.

'Please, Mary, I'm begging you!'

Suddenly, Dorwina popped out from behind the cubicle and addressed Lisa. 'Lisa, get a hold of yourself and fight it.'

I impulsively yelled out, 'Let her go wash her hands!'

Dorwina just stared at me.

'James, I know you mean well but stay out of this,' said Mary.

I don't know what possessed me, but I walked over to Lisa's chair and said, 'There are no germs under your seat. Watch me touch it.'

I slowly moved my hands towards her seat, but I couldn't touch it. Hard as I tried, I could not do it!

'See, there are germs under the seat,' said Lisa.

They took Lisa out of group as all eyes were on me. I had opened my big mouth, but I hadn't delivered. I had not only let Lisa down, but all my fellow patients too. A few moments later, group was dismissed.

My fellow patients kind of gathered around in little cliques. It seems strange to me that everyone, no matter how weird – killers, jailbirds and even retarded people – form a clique. If you put man-eating cannibals together, they'd form a clique.

I decided to lay low after my fiasco in group.

I noticed a computer as I walked around the house. I wanted to check my email, but Barney was on it. He smiled every time I walked by. He knew I wanted to use it. I decided Barney was the type of guy who would only get off the computer if you asked him to. I wasn't going to give him that pleasure. I ignored him and walked up to my room.

The guy from Philly was sitting there on his bed with headphones on. Thank God I got this shy guy for a roommate. I could hear the gay guy talking over in the next room. I could tell he would have driven me crazy. I started to think about tomorrow: Telegraph Avenue. Just then Philly jumped up and yelled, 'I'm sorry! I didn't mean it!' Then he sat down and covered his face.

'Are you OK, Philly?'

'Yeah. I get these thoughts. Like I just raped or killed someone.'

He plugged the earphones back in and went to sleep. The gay guy suddenly became more appealing.

TELEGRAPH AVENUE

The next morning I was up on time and sitting down for coffee. I normally didn't drink coffee, but I normally didn't get up early, either. I'm not a morning person. The hyper girl came and sat down beside me.

'Hi, I'm Anna. You're James, right?'

I nodded and looked the other way. It didn't work – she went off like I was her long-lost best friend. She'd say something, and then go off laughing to herself.

'Don't you just love the morning, James?'

'No, I hate the morning.'

'Oh, James, I treat every morning like it is a new day.'

'Every morning IS a new day!' I said.

Unfortunately, that didn't deter her. She kept chattering until I said, 'Hey, you should try the decaf.'

'Oh, James. You're so funny! We're going to be good friends, I can tell.'

Just then Harry yelled out, 'Group! Everyone in here for group.'

I never thought I would be this happy for group.

Everyone hurried out of the dining room and grabbed a seat. The fat guy came swaying in a few moments late. One by one every patient told his or her plan for the day. Lisa's plan was to sit on the bathroom floor for 20 minutes. Now this was a girl I felt sorry for. Everyone used that one little bathroom and let me tell you, when 20 people use the same bathroom without any sprays, it stinks! I hated going in there. Every time I used it, I flashed back to the city jail in Shreveport, Louisiana.

I had got so drunk one night I blacked out and woke up in a cell to the sound of some guy pissing on the commode. Unfortunately, my face was stationed beneath it. Urine ricocheted across my face because I was too sick to move my head. I found out later a couple came over to press charges because I'd tried to assault them in a bar. I guess the good news was that, after seeing how pathetic I looked, they decided to let the matter drop. To this day, I don't remember going to any bar in Shreveport, Louisiana.

As the patients told their plans, I was a little disappointed. I had seen all these movies where people spill their guts in group therapies and I wanted some of that here. I guess the OCD was so dominant in all of us that it made it almost impossible to relate to each other on a deeper level. One girl was afraid of crowds. Her plan was to walk around the mall. Another guy was afraid of public conveniences, so he was going down to Telegraph Avenue to touch the toilets.

When it came to me, I just said I wasn't going to ask for reassurance more than three times at Telegraph Avenue. Again, everyone wanted to know: reassurance about what? I didn't trust anyone enough for that yet. I wondered if any of the counsellors knew my problems. The therapists were the only ones who had to know your problems; the counsellors only knew if you told them.

Those of us bound for Telegraph Avenue piled into a van. I sat in the back as Anna grabbed a seat up front, continuing to chatter. I got as far away from her as I could. When we reached Telegraph Avenue, we split off in pairs, but I got to go solo. Each of us was assigned a counsellor to check in with every 15 minutes to see how he or she was doing. I told my counsellor, Mark, a nice-looking guy about 25, that I would be OK by myself. He then asked me my OCD. 'I don't care to say,' I said. He told me 'whatever' and we agreed to meet in 15 minutes in front of the big academic bookstore.

Telegraph Avenue (or just 'Telegraph', to those in the know) is a unique place. You have a bewildering mix of smart, rich preppies from Berkeley, 'ethnics' such as Asian students and Hispanic and Latino immigrants, burnt-out hippy throwbacks from California's flower-power scene and rich men- and women-about-town shopping and eating out in swanky restaurants. It's also full of druggies and homeless people, who mainly gang together in People's Park, but also hang out on the Avenue to hawk, beg and buy their daily provisions. The whole area has a mad, surreal Bohemian atmosphere.

I wandered about until I saw this attractive Hispanic girl looking at a newspaper. I approached her. 'Hey, miss, you looking for a job?'

She turned around with an amazed look on her face. 'Yes, I am. How did you know?'

I was on the verge of telling her it was because she was looking at the classifieds, but she was attractive, young and had a sexy accent. So I did what I had to: 'I'm psychic,' I said.

'Great. You psychic, you can tell me where to find job.'

Oh boy, my bullshit had backfired on me. I looked up at the clock on the bank as I pondered my response to the señorita. Mark was somewhere in the vicinity and I didn't want him to catch me hitting on this girl. A second later he seemed to appear out of nowhere and spoke.

'Hey, James, what's up?'

My mind started going again. I was fast on my feet and quickly turned away from the girl.

'This girl is homeless and I was trying to shake hands with her.'

'What's your OCD?' Mark asked.

I didn't really want to tell him but I had no choice.

'I'm afraid of drugs and being around anyone who might use them.'

He told me good job and to meet him at the van in 15 minutes. That was close. I told him not to tell any other counsellor about my OCD and he agreed. I could tell he was a nice guy and had a feeling he would keep his word.

The Hispanic girl asked me what kind of work I did. I pondered a moment, and then told the lie I would be telling the whole time I was at Triumph. 'I'm a writer doing research on the homeless. Me and 20 people are living together in a big house all doing research together on the homeless.'

'That's good,' she said. 'Is that boy doing research with you?'

'Of course.'

She looked up and smiled at me. 'Can I get job in research?'

'Well, maybe after I train you,' I said.

Oh, such a sweet girl. I think that's why I always tried to meet Latinos and Asian women. It's not that they're gullible; it's just that they're so pure and innocent. I decided if I ever got cured, I would settle down with one of them.

I found out the girl's name was Ray Ray. I told her that if there was an opening at the research centre, I would get in touch with her. Of course, I had to have a way to get in touch with her about that opening, right? I got her email address.

I walked back to the van with mixed feelings. I'd met an attractive girl, but I hadn't done anything to help my disease. That bothered me a lot. The good thing was I'd get another chance that afternoon. We would go back to Telegraph after lunch.

We had another nice lunch and, to my surprise, I didn't have any trouble eating. The big fat guy even remarked that the ice tea tasted funny and asked what was in it. Just a few days ago that would have freaked me out. Maybe just coming here had given me some confidence. I even grabbed the pitcher, filled my glass up and drank it all in one swoop! I got up after that feeling great.

I told the big guy thanks and he just looked around, baffled. I grabbed an apple and headed for the computer. Barney must have seen me because he tried to jump in front of me. We ended up running into each other and he lost his balance, landing head first in the trashcan. Mary heard the fall and came rushing in.

'What happened?' she said.

With a big grin on my face I said, 'I know Barney is afraid of germs so I was helping him to do some exposure.'

Barney was furious. 'No, you pushed me!'

Truth was I didn't push him any more than he pushed me. But if this is how he saw it I thought it might come in handy in the future, i.e. the fear factor. He might now think twice before attacking my vulnerabilities in group or anywhere else. I quickly went with the flow and said, 'Tonya said we were supposed to help and encourage each other with our obsessions.'

Now Mary was a sweet girl but clearly not the brightest in her class.

'I'm sure James was just trying to help you, Barney.'

Mary took Barney to the bathroom to clean up. I checked my emails.

The next class started about 15 minutes later. A new

counsellor was running this class. She was quite beautiful and exotic. We started with telling how high our anxiety had got in the morning exposure. Most of the patients said their anxiety got to seven or eight and now it was three, four or five. Some of the hard-cores said a ten and now they were an eight. That girl, Anna, the one who was wired all the time, gave herself this score. I looked at her and she was laughing and carrying on like she was at a party. I knew right then and there that some of these patients didn't know what real anxiety was. Real anxiety is when you put a paper bag over your head to keep from hyperventilating. Or when a gun is pointed in your face – and you're the one holding it. Now that's real anxiety.

When it was my turn, I wussed out. I pretended my anxiety peaked at seven and now was a five. I wanted to go back to Telegraph, and I was afraid if I said my anxiety only got to a four or five they might not let me go back. Besides, I wanted to see Ray Ray again.

I found out later I would be catching the bus to Telegraph Avenue this time, and that the bus stop was only a short block away. The other patients were going to the mall and would have counsellors with them, but since I was the only one going to Telegraph, I would be going solo. I also found out that we would be playing basketball at the Triumph gym that night with some of the doctors and patients from present and past. Dr Swenson, they said, was out of town and wouldn't be able to play. I was in luck since I was a bit intimidated by the thought of meeting him. After all, he'd been on some TV show in which he'd talked a guy into coming out of a closet who'd been in there a year because of his obsession about germ contamination. So he had to be something special, right?

The bus stop was right in front of a great doughnut shop.

The bus ran every 20 minutes so I decided to get a doughnut to pass the time. As I walked in, I spotted an Asian girl sitting by the window looking out. I walked over to her table and asked her if I could join her. She agreed. Within seconds I was laying my spiel. I was doing research on homeless people and I was an actor.

It was true that I was an actor, to a degree. My first stab at it had been prompted by a movie I saw on the telly one night when I was drunk most of the time, living off my mother in Florida. The movie was the true story of James Dean. I was fascinated by this man who was very complex, just like me – mean yet sensitive. He had many layers, like me. Next thing I knew I was off to California to be an actor. Unfortunately, I made a stop in Lake Tahoe and spent the thousand dollars my mother had given me on booze, broads and gambling. A few days later I was broke, except for twenty dollars, and was preparing for my shameful trip back to Florida. That would all change after a chance encounter. I somehow wandered into the audience of a celebrity tennis tournament in my usual state of intoxication and, lo and behold, Clint Eastwood was playing. I saw all the attention Clint was getting and that reminded me of the real reason why I wanted to be an actor: I was looking for the attention I'd never got as a child. I knew this was a bad reason, but that didn't stop me. I saw him exit toward some cabins after the match and I ran over to meet him. We exchanged a few words and that evening I was on the Greyhound bus to Hollywood.

I managed to live in Hollywood for a while and even got one or two breaks on TV dramas, along with some other stuff. My problem was I acted more like an agent. I snuck into the studios every day and talked my way into offices, meeting important people. The only good thing that came out of it was that I met Mel Brooks. Mel walked up to me one day at Twentieth Century Fox studios and said, 'Are you fricking insane?'

'No. Why do you ask?'

'Because you're here every fricking day with the same fricking clothes on!'

He warned me that if he'd noticed me, then sooner or later security would notice me too. Mel was right. At that time I had one cheap suit that I'd bought on Hollywood Boulevard somewhere and I wore it every time I went to the studio. He was also right about the other thing.

Mel and I ended up being friends: telephone friends, to be more precise. We have talked every few months for the last 20 years. He always encourages me. Many times I've been suicidal when I've called, and he's snapped me out of it. Of course, I never told him about the suicidal episodes at the time. Mel is a special kind of person, no doubt.

Getting back to the girl in the doughnut shop, I laid all my lines on her and finally let her speak.

'Nice to meet you, James. I'm a doctor doing research at Triumph Hospital.'

'Uh, good. I see my bus. Have a good one!'

Thank God the bus drove up. I finally got to Telegraph Avenue, but not before I tried to pick up a Korean girl on the bus. Unfortunately, she was married. On Telegraph, I noticed this black punker guy with a red Mohawk, begging just up from the bus stop. Good person to practise my exposure on, I thought. I got nervous as I walked closer to him. What was I going to say?

'Sir. Do you know where a shelter is, because I'm homeless.'

He just looked at me for a while. My anxiety shot up. Why in the hell did I say sir?

'You don't look homeless. You got any 'erb?' he said.

My mind began to spin. What was I going to say?

Suddenly, out of nowhere, this beautiful Asian girl walked past me towards the academic bookstore. I watched her, mesmerised. I told the homeless punker that I was going to bum a cigarette and would be back. I quickly detoured over to the academic bookstore. I knew it was the cowardly way out but I did it anyway.

The academic bookstore was a beautiful place with three floors and a coffee shop. I found her standing in line and wiggled my way into the line right behind her. I started my usual chat that I was a writer and that I was doing research. The girl was from Japan and going to law school at Berkeley. I bought her a cup of coffee and sat down and chatted. She was so beautiful I was happy just to look at her. Before I knew it, time had passed and I had to be getting back to the house. I got her email and made a date to meet her at a restaurant that was right down the street.

As I walked out of the bookstore, I felt terrible guilt. I was starting to feel at home on Telegraph Avenue, but only because I kept wasting my exposure time talking to women. I had to do something to make up for it. The punk rocker was still there begging. I started to walk right by him. I hesitated. I stopped and reached out my hand to him.

'Hi, I'm Jimbo, nice to meet you.'

We shook hands and a moment later I had jumped onto a bus. I grinned all the way back to the house.

BASKETBALL

We all walked over to the gym together. I hadn't played basketball in years. I had played in high school for a small-town team in Louisiana. I was second string on a lousy team. That should tell you something. I wondered if the gay guy was going to play. Everybody had to go to the gym. The gay guy and this tall, attractive, brunette patient just walked around giggling. I had to admit I was jealous. They appeared not to have a care in the world. It seemed more like they were here just for a rest – like this was one of those Beverly Hills spas.

I went out and started shooting baskets. I noticed there were a lot of new guys here. I hadn't seen any of them at Within Reach. Bob, the night-shift counsellor, explained to me that some were doctors from Triumph and some were ex-patients of Within Reach.

As we were warming up, a man came rushing over to me and yelled, 'Hey, you look just like Timothy Leary!'

I froze. My anxiety shot up to a ten.

I ran after the man, who was now under the basket shooting. 'What did you mean by that?'

'By what?'

'Saying I look like Timothy Leary.'

'Timothy Leary was the first acid head.'

That was not the answer I wanted. My mind started racing. The man took off dribbling. I tried grabbing hold of myself, but I couldn't. I chased him down again.

'Sir, do I look like I'm on drugs?'

He looked around a moment, then responded to another, younger player. 'Doesn't he look like Timothy Leary?'

Desperately, I grabbed the man. 'Why? Do I look spaced out? Is that why you said that?' I said.

'Timothy Leary was a distinguished-looking man. Especially when he was younger. He was a sharp guy. A Harvard professor!'

The anxiety started to go down, but after I shot a couple of baskets, it came back. I ran over to the man again.

'Are you sure you didn't mean I was on drugs?'

The man smiled. 'No, I don't think you're on drugs, but

only you know for sure. I can see you have some problems.'

I grabbed the basketball from his hands and drove in for a shot. In a small way it was funny. Here I was, terrified of drugs and, from that man's point of view, along with thousands of others I had met in my life who didn't really know me, I acted like a guy on drugs. Kind of ironic, wasn't it?

We picked up teams by shooting free throws. Barney was on the opposite team. Thank God Barney didn't know my problem. If he found out, I thought, I'd be at his mercy. I tried to ignore Barney and the man who'd commented on me by just standing under the basket. That quickly changed when I heard the tall girl yell, 'Barney, you just made a touchdown against James!'

Then, of course, Barney yells out, 'It's easy because James is such a wimp!'

I angrily grabbed the ball from one of my teammates and took off, dribbling towards the basket where Barney and the Leary guy stood, awaiting my arrival. With all my strength, I went for a lay-up between them. I knocked them both to the ground as I went up for the shot. I missed it, but immediately grabbed the rebound and put it back in. I turned and looked at the two lying on the court.

'You ready to play some ball?'

After that I was knocking people all over the place. I even knocked the fat guy down. I felt a little bad about him. But not that bad. After a few games, we stopped for the night. The Leary man came over and shook my hand.

'Hey, you were an animal out there.'

I thanked him. I went over to Barney and shook hands. Now, Barney wasn't a very good basketball player but he was out there scrapping with everyone else. It finally hit me that we were all here for the same reason: to get better.

DR SWENSON

The next morning I was sore all over. I was looking forward, though, to seeing the famous Dr Swenson. I also realised that just because I ate with the other patients and had shaken hands with a punker, that didn't mean I was all better. That experience with the man on the basketball court brought me back to reality. I had a long way to go.

I walked up to Dr Swenson's door. It was partly open. Should I just walk in? I thought better of it and knocked on the door. A voice yelled out at me.

'If you're a nose-picker, a butt-scratcher or a hand-washer, I'm too busy to see you!'

I heard laughter and a moment later a basketball came flying through, forcing the door open. I'll be damned! It was the Leary man from the basketball game. I knew right then and there, no matter what happened, I was going to like this man.

'Why didn't you tell me who you were last night?' I said.

'I didn't know it was you.'

'Come on, Doc! That Timothy Leary crap?'

'That was pure coincidence. I knew something was wrong when you kept asking me for reassurance.'

I told the Doc all my weird problems and he said he was familiar with some of them. My OCD kicked in again. I wanted to ask him again about last night. Was it really just coincidence? It's hell how something goes over and over and over in your mind. I was unable to focus on anything he was saying. Finally, I broke down. I needed reassurance and I needed it fast.

'Dr Swenson, was it really just coincidence last night?'

He slowly shook his head. 'James, if I tell you again, a couple minutes from now, your OCD will start up again and you won't be sure what I told you. You'll want me to repeat it again and again.'

'Doc,' I said. 'I will get on the floor and lick your shoes if you just make this anxiety go away.'

I knew the Doc was right. But I couldn't stop the 'what if' that kept going over in my mind.

'Doc, there have been times when I would've committed suicide if somebody hadn't given me reassurance and made me feel the anxiety literally leaving my body.'

The Doc just looked at me.

'Please, Doc, just one more time!'

'Fight it, James. Just like your life depended on it, and it does.'

I was trembling like so many times before. The Doc said changing the subject would help. I asked him if it wasn't paranoia. He told me that a paranoid person wouldn't ask for reassurance; he or she would just assume you'd harmed them in some way and move on to their next delusion. A person with OCD knows their fears are irrational even though a part of them keeps saying, 'What if?'

I let all that sink in before responding honestly.

'Doc, sometimes I don't think my fears are irrational.'

The Doc looked around the room. It was an awkward moment. I didn't have to be a shrink to know there was no great answer for what I just said. I quickly changed the subject. Maybe because I didn't want an answer.

'Hey, Doc, I am an actor and did a movie for PBS and Masterpiece Theatre and I am a friend of Mel Brooks!'

He asked me how I knew him and I told him how we met at the studios.

'Good, James, but speaking of that and using a showbiz term, I heard you didn't make a "good entrance" here.'

Oh, Lord. I knew he had read Tonya's notes.

'Sorry, Doc. I was just so nervous about coming here. Besides, I don't think Tonya likes me either as I kind of insulted her during our session.'

'She didn't mention that in the notes. Don't you think she would have mentioned that if she didn't like you, James?'

He was right, but I didn't want to think about it and quickly changed the subject again. I asked the Doc if anybody else had been to Within Reach with my problem and got cured. He told me yes. Of course, he would say that no matter what. Hell, I would tell a patient that too. Got to give a guy a little hope, right?

'What kind of relationship do you have with your mother, James?'

I suddenly felt uncomfortable. 'I don't want to talk about that, Doc.'

After my mother had given me up, I never trusted women. I blamed her for that, and for every other problem I ever had. In reality I hated myself, and took it out on her.

I quickly changed the subject and a few moments later I was headed 'home': to Telegraph Avenue.

IMPULSIVE

A few days went by and I continued to meet women during my exposure time at Telegraph. I knew I had to do something about it. I had another meeting with Dr Swenson. I was debating how to handle it when I sat down in his office.

'Hey, Doc, there's another problem I have. Whenever I see an attractive woman, I immediately run over and talk to her.'

The Doc smiled. 'Good for you. Most guys with OCD wouldn't have the confidence to do that.'

'Yeah, Doc, it would be fine. But, uh – I have to.'

'What do you mean, have to?'

'I see an attractive woman, and I have no choice. I don't mean any harm to the girls. But I get some kick out of just talking to them.'

The Doctor explained to me that that wasn't OCD. That was about impulse control. He said it would be fine if I wanted to meet someone but if I had to, that was a problem.

'I didn't think it was OCD, because OCD causes you discomfort. These women give me enjoyment,' I said.

'But do you want people you work with, for instance, to say you're weird? How about having a girlfriend or even a wife. How could they put up with that?' said Dr Swenson.

He was right. He also told me that, in some strange way, it functioned similarly to my OCD: it was like a drug. The feeling I got from reassurance was like a fix, and the high I got from approaching women was the same. I knew he was right. But at the end of the session, he really scared the hell out of me with his final statement. 'James, if you can't get this women thing under control, we'll have to send you home.'

My heart dropped. I knew this was my last chance in life.

'Oh, don't worry – it's under control.'

'You know, James, I would think you'd be afraid to approach strange women with your OCD. You'd be afraid they would say something to give you an anxiety attack.'

'Doc, the impulse is so strong, I take the risk.'

He shook his head in amazement and told me that, the next time I went to Telegraph, I should sit by an attractive girl on the bus and under no circumstances should I speak to her. He also mentioned I had to tell Tonya about this.

Of course, that meant that if I didn't, he would.

I agreed to his plan and soon after I was walking towards the doughnut shop. I tried to think about the other patients.

I wanted to care about them, but I was so self-absorbed with my own problems that it was almost impossible. I didn't notice anybody who was really suffering, other than this short little chubby guy. I believe his name was Larry. He was cute like a little teddy bear. He shook like he was about to have an anxiety attack – or worse, like he was having one all the time. I heard him say his OCD was hanging around the toilet to make sure he flushed it. After he flushed, he would walk away a few steps then turn back and recheck. He could do it for hours. I think hanging around the crapper would give anybody anxiety. But to tell you the truth I wished that that was my OCD.

On my trip to Telegraph Avenue I decided to try Dr Swenson's therapy. Once I entered the bus, I noticed a very attractive Chinese girl. When she saw me looking at her, she smiled. I slowly walked down the aisle and sat next to her. I wanted to say hello and even felt my lips begin to open. I had to grab a hold of myself before it was too late. I covered my mouth and began to curse myself for being so weak. I've never tried heroin, and have never gone 'cold turkey', but I can't imagine any greater anxiety than what I was feeling.

I tried looking out of the window and counting the stops. My hands were shaking and my legs were trembling. 'Five more stops,' I said to myself as we got closer and closer. Finally, I could see Telegraph Avenue in the distance. 'Yes! One more stop,' I shouted out under my breath.

'Are you talking to me?' said the girl. I quickly shook my head. I was almost there . . .

'Hello, miss. Where are you from?'

RAGE

I got the girl's email address and went on my way. I had given in to my impulse, but I justified it by saying I was here for OCD and not some silly impulse control involving girls. I went back to the spot where I'd seen the punk-rocker guy and he was there again. He also had some other odd-looking street people with him. I felt very uncomfortable. I realised they were a lot younger than me, and I was dressed much more like an old preppie.

I had to have a way in. I pondered this. A moment later I ran over to the convenience store and bought four cans of soda. I walked up to the punkers and offered them all one.

'Hey, remember me from yesterday? Jimbo, remember?'

The big punker looked at me without speaking. My mind started racing. I blurted out, 'Yeah, I just bummed five bucks from some rich little preppie from Berkeley and I thought I'd share the wealth.'

'Cool,' said the big punker. 'I'm Rage.'

They quickly tore open the sodas and one of the younger punks said, 'Thanks, pops. I'll get you high sometime for this.'

Rage shook my hand and introduced me to the others. I was so nervous I didn't hear their names. My mind started racing again, thinking about all the drug-ridden hands I had just shaken. During anxiety attack 1001 it occurred to me that maybe they'd be so flattered by my donation they might invite me to join the flock. Of course, the initiation would be, at the very least, sharing a joint. My mind then quickly went to my compulsion. I needed to go and wash my hands at the academic bookstore.

Suddenly, my ego jumped into the mix and my mind was off and running about the little pimple-faced bastard who'd called me pops! I wanted to grab him right there and wring his neck. The Doc had said something about postponing my compulsions for a while by thinking about something else. My anger at the kid was doing it.

'You got any cinnamon, Jimbo?' said Rage.

'What?' I said.

'Yeah, I snorted some last night, Jimbo, and it really zonked me out.'

I don't know what I was thinking but for some reason I blurted out, 'Sorry, Rage, I used my last batch for some cinnamon toast last night!'

All the punks broke into laughter except one: Rage. He stared straight at me before grabbing my shirt collar with his big right hand.

I began to tremble as he slowly began to speak. 'Did you get a buzz, Jimbo?'

'Uh, yeah.'

Rage smiled and let go of my shirt. As strange as this sounds, I wasn't afraid of this intimidating giant of a man. I was too busy looking at his hands.

Suddenly, a beautiful Japanese woman walked by us. I started to go after her but I made myself stay put. I might have still been in shock from my Rage encounter. Of course, that didn't keep my eyes from following her as she crossed the street and went in the academic bookstore.

'You cold, pops, because you're shaking like a leaf?' said the young punk.

I wanted to slap the kid but he gave me a way out that I couldn't pass up. I told the punks I was going to the academic bookstore to bum some coffee to warm me up.

'Sorry we can't go with,' said Rage. 'We're not allowed in there.'

I jolted towards the bookstore after hearing the good news

from Rage. I went upstairs and saw the beauty drinking coffee. I quickly decided my hands could wait. I walked over to her.

'Hey, are you from Japan?'

'Yes. How did you know?'

I grabbed a seat and told her I used to live in Tokyo and could spot a Japanese girl anywhere and that I had just returned to LA to resume my writing career. I explained to her I was in Berkeley on assignment, doing research on the homeless.

She seemed impressed.

'Where did you live in Tokyo?' she said.

She had me on that one. All I really knew about Japan was Godzilla.

'By the airport,' I blurted out.

'Did you ever get a chance to go to Osaka and Universal studios?' she asked.

'Of course,' I said.

I looked at my watch. I realised I had to catch the bus back soon. I got the girl's email address and told her I'd like to meet her again. I ran down the bookstore's steps and, before I could hit the exit door, I spotted another cute Asian girl browsing in the romance section. I knew I didn't have time but I couldn't help myself and quickly went over to her.

'You must be romantic,' I said. The girl shyly asked me how I knew. I used the psychic line again – hey, I couldn't help myself. She then told me she was from Osaka. 'I used to work at Universal Studios there,' I said.

'Willy?' she said. 'I used to go there all the time!'

'Hey, I love the way you Japanese say "Willy" instead of "really".'

Of course, I had said that to change the subject. I told her I had an appointment and quickly got her email address before she could ask me anything more about Osaka. A moment later I was leaving the store when I heard her yell out, 'Where did you live in Osaka?'

Without blinking an eye, I said, 'By the airport.'

I got to the bus stop just as the bus pulled up. I started thinking about how I'd promised the Doc that I would stop all this nonsense with women. I angrily turned away from the bus and headed back to Telegraph. Rage was there with a skinny guy sporting a purple Mohawk. Before I could speak, he introduced himself as Jazz and told me he was so skinny because he hadn't eaten in weeks and could I spare a dollar.

'You faggot. This is Jimbo. He's one of us,' said Rage.

'Oh. Sorry, dude. Hey, you got a quarter, Jimbo?' said Jazz.

Rage popped Jazz across the head as I handed him a quarter. I knew the next bus would be here soon and time was a-wasting so I looked straight at Rage and said, 'You got a smoke?'

I knew Rage hadn't seen a shower in a long time as he handed me a cigarette and lit it with his lighter. I tried to look cool, even inhaling and praying the whole time that I wouldn't start coughing and choking in front of them. I made a few seconds of small talk before telling them I was supposed to meet someone about a deal down the road.

When I got back to the bus stop, I took one last puff and handed the rest to a homeless man. A big smile broke across my face. If I hadn't talked to those girls, I wouldn't have touched, let alone smoked, the cigarette Rage had given me. I was compensating for my guilt by trying something especially risky. I was also sure that the Doc and Tonya would never be putting this method into their 'How to' book. But hey, whatever works. It also hit me that I hadn't washed my hands!

THE NEW PATIENT

I got lucky. Tonya was writing me up when I came bustling through the front door. I told her it wasn't my fault, that I'd met this homeless guy who'd caused me so much intense anxiety that I'd decided to stay and push it to the limit. Tonya was ecstatic that I'd hung in there, and decided not to write me up. Of course, I didn't really know what getting written up really meant. I was sure there were consequences though.

I walked into the next group and sat down. A few moments later I heard one of the counsellors announce that the new patient had arrived. A moment later she walked in. I was deeply disappointed. She was black.

Now, you have to remember I spent my teenage years in a small town in Louisiana. The whites live on the south side of town and the blacks live on the north side. I tried not to dislike blacks when I was growing up. I brought a black friend to my sister's house once, and my brother-in-law told me not to come back.

I'm sure everyone is racist to a degree. If you put a lie detector on anyone, black or white, you'll find racism. Whenever a group of whites get together in my town, the 'n' word will come up. I'm also sure if you get a group of blacks together, 'that no good whitey' will be heard.

The new patient, whose name was Alley, was tall and very black. I decided to just keep my distance, as I never was attracted to black women. Alley stood up to tell us about herself. She was from Oregon. She'd graduated from UCLA and was going to be an English professor before her OCD had kicked in.

We broke for supper after her introduction. I had mostly kept quiet at the other meals but I remembered one of the therapists telling us to do the opposite of what we normally did at home. If all we did back home was watch television, then we should do the opposite here. I decided to take their advice. I sat listening, waiting for a chance to join the conversation.

The topic was Ted Kennedy and how great he was for our country and how he helped the downtrodden. Everyone was falling over everyone else to agree. I knew I was going to regret this, but I jumped in.

'Ted Kennedy is nothing but a drunken buffoon! He doesn't even know who Sammy Sosa and Mark McGwire are. He called them Soosa and Mack McGuire. He let that young woman die, too, didn't he?'

Wow, did it get quiet! I felt like a hurricane was coming. You know that eerie quiet before the storm hits? A moment later, it did, as counsellors and patients alike spouted comments from every direction.

'If it wasn't for Ted Kennedy, there would be no help for starving families!'

'Ted Kennedy cares about the little person, James!'

'If it wasn't for Ted Kennedy, places like Triumph wouldn't even exist to help people like us!'

The new girl, in the eye of the storm, stood up in the middle and calmly pronounced, 'I don't agree with James, but he has a right to his opinion.'

The room got quiet again. I got up and walked into the front room to wait for the last class of the evening. I'd known what I was saying back there was going to cause trouble. I'm sure that's why I did it. Sabotage again. I'm not a good person so I don't deserve friends. Truth be known, I felt sorry for Teddy Kennedy: all the heartache he and his family had to deal with – unbelievable.

I popped back into the computer room and found Teddy

Bear sitting by himself. He was shaking again. I genuinely felt sorry for him, too. I pondered a moment, trying to think of the right thing to say. He caught me off guard by speaking to me first.

'You like the Rangers, James?'

'Uh, yeah,' I said.

'Arnie likes the Rangers too.'

'Who's Arnie?' I asked.

'Your roommate!'

I felt bad. I hadn't even taken the time to find out my roommate's name. I thought that maybe I should try to be nicer to everyone, so I said, 'Teddy Bear, I love hockey more than life itself!'

Whoops. I'd forgotten that he didn't know I called him that. But he just smiled – I guess nicknames didn't matter much when you were severely anxious most of the time. He nodded in agreement about the hockey. I didn't give a rat's ass about the game, but I thought by pretending to it might cheer up the little fuzz ball, and it did.

A moment later Barney entered the room. 'Are you crazy, James? Attacking a liberal like Teddy Kennedy in Berkeley!'

'Sabotage,' I said.

He asked me what I meant by that and I told him nothing and changed the subject. 'Hey, you see that new girl being all diplomatic and goody-two-shocs with the counsellors, Barney?'

'She was doing you a favour,' said Barney.

'Yeah, you're right. I wonder what her motives were?'

'Not everyone has a motive, James.'

I felt uncomfortable and changed the subject, again. I asked Barney what kinds of meds he was on. He told me he was taking an amphetamine-like stimulant, among others, and I found that curious. Anna was on the same stuff, and she and Barney were the most wired people in the house. Why were they taking a drug that some junkies scored for kicks? I supposed it must have somehow calmed down people who were already manic. But Anna and Barney were like hamsters on speed! God knows what they must have been like off it.

I decided to call it a night and told Barney I would see him in the morning. He asked me if I was heading off to bed and I said yes.

'You're off now, James?'

I told him yes again.

'You're going up the stairs now, James?'

'OCD, Barney?' I asked.

He nodded yes and started to ask me again, so I flew up the stairs before he could finish.

I had come to the conclusion after being at Within Reach for a short while that everybody connects anything and everything with OCD. Fart too much: OCD. Don't fart: OCD. Wipe your butt too much: OCD. Don't wipe your butt at all: OCD!

HIGH TIMES

After dinner I got into trouble with Dorwina. I was sitting in the living room when she came in and said, 'Are you going to let Barney and Larry do the entire kitchen clean-up?'

I didn't know what she meant, so I said, 'What the hell are you talking about?'

She informed me that I was on the list to do clean-up. I didn't even know there was a list. I angrily stormed into the kitchen and no one was in there. I peeked into the dining room and Barney was blabbing away to somebody. Teddy

Bear, meanwhile, was nowhere to be found. I ended up doing all the dishes myself.

A short time later Dorwina popped back into the kitchen and said. 'You should try and work as a team when doing clean-up.'

My anger began to build. I wanted to insult this woman, but how? She was beautiful from head to toe. I would even go so far as to say that she resembled a movie star. That said, if someone were to have given me a microscope and demanded I find a flaw . . . I guess I could have said that her nose was just a tad long. I quickly decided that a girl this vain would be bothered by any remark to that effect.

'Hey, Dorwina, I used to be an "actor", and you know what they say about an actor with a big nose?' I pointed at my nose and continued without giving her any chance to reply. 'They say you have "CHARACTER"! Now, on the other hand, Dorwina, if YOU were an actress, they would just say, "YOU HAVE A BIG NOSE"!'

I laughed out loud at my triumph. I could not describe accurately the look she gave me back. You would've had to be there to appreciate it. I quickly ran into the other room to gloat about it with the other patients. Of course, I knew there would be consequences in one way or another. So be it. I knew one thing for certain: I didn't like Dorwina. But even worse: she didn't like me.

I shared my triumph with Barney. It went down well, but he became too manic about it and wouldn't shut up. I had heard through the grapevine that he'd got kicked out before. It had something to do with his lack of self-control.

After that I went back into the television room and tried to mingle. I really didn't feel comfortable with anyone except maybe the guy from Philly and Teddy Bear. Speaking of Philly, he had told me that they were showing him slasher movies in order to try to desensitise him from his violent thoughts. The poor guy was so hypersensitive that he would freak if anyone walked close by him. 'I didn't bump you, did I? I am so sorry if I did!' You would hear this in one form or another throughout the day. Truth was, he wouldn't harm a flea.

The next morning I was sitting in Tonya's office spilling the beans. 'Tonya, I told Dr Swenson about a little problem I have with women. He told me to discuss it with you. I have to talk to every pretty woman I see.'

Tonya looked befuddled. I hoped she didn't think I was hitting on her, so I quickly added, 'Of course, I don't do that to professional people, like all the attractive staff we have working here. I'm very glad about that because you're a very attractive woman, Tonya.'

Tonya seemed to really enjoy my last statement.

'Of course, I have to admit, I am a bit of a con man.'

Now that I had her head spinning, I quickly changed the subject. 'Hey, Tonya, I was thinking, I need a prop of some kind to fit in with the street people. I was thinking about that magazine, *High Times*.'

'I want to hear more about the women thing, James.'

My plan hadn't worked.

'Well, Tonya, I've been talking to all the women at Telegraph.'

'Maybe you should go somewhere else for your exposure.'

Oh no! I was crazy about Telegraph. I wasn't going to give it up that easily. 'Tonya, I made a promise to myself last night that I would ignore the women at Telegraph. I came here to get better and nothing will get in the way!'

'I don't know, James.'

'Listen, Tonya, I'm the one who told you and the Doc. It was my decision, right?'

Tonya pondered a moment. I quickly told her I tended to sabotage anything I did. I wasn't worthy to be here. They should have chosen someone else. I wasn't a good person and didn't deserve this chance, so they should kick me out. I told her I did the same thing with women. If I met a girl who was conservative, I'd start talking about sex. If I found a girl who was very open-minded and ended up in the sack with her, then she was no good and had no morals. If the girl was a minority, I would say something ethnic to offend her. I told Tonya I'd tried to figure out why I did this to myself. I'd come up with the fact that my mother gave me up when I was five and chose to keep my sister, so I must have had a major defect. 'So, Tonya, no one ever loved me. Not as a boy and not as a man. I came into the world alone and I will die alone,' I said in finishing.

Tonya looked as if she was searching for something profound to say, so I quickly cut her off.

'I don't want to talk about this any more!'

'OK, James. You go buy *High Times* at the news-stand and walk around Telegraph. Make sure you go into the Park this time, too, because you'll get loads of exposure there. Go sit by some druggies and let them see you reading it. By the way, James, *High Times* is a great idea. How did you come up with that?'

'Actually, Tonya, it came from an incident I had when I saw a *Time* magazine cover. It had a young girl on it with a pill in her mouth and the heading read "What Ecstasy Does to Your Brain". I looked at it from a distance before finally getting the nerve to touch the picture of the pill. A moment later I felt somehow I was going to get high from having touched it. I walked in and out of the store trying to calm myself down. I came to the conclusion that I could only get relief by washing my hands in the men's room. When I finally made it home, it dawned on me that I had touched both the inside and outside door handles of the store with my contaminated hands. For the next couple of weeks I would have to stand and wait for someone to open the door for me to enter. Of course, exiting brought on the same problem. I finally went there late one night after closing time and washed the front door. From then on I only had to wait for someone leaving to slip out of the door unharmed. I had to steer well clear of that *Time* magazine, though, the whole time it was on the shelves.'

'It was just a picture, James.'

I nodded in agreement. Truth was, that had happened just a few weeks back and I was only now realising how crazy it was. I was definitely on the right track.

'Hey, Tonya, why are we allowed visitors?' I blurted out, randomly.

'James, this is not a psychiatric ward. There are no bars here. No one signed any of you in here. You are all adults and can walk out of this place at any time you choose. It's your decision. But if you stay here all we ask is that you follow a few simple rules.'

I nodded again.

'Keep up the good work, James,' added Tonya.

I walked out of the door wondering if I'd conned her or she'd conned me. It also dawned on me that Dorwina hadn't told anyone about my insult. If she had, it would have been in Tonya's notes. I had no idea she was that vain. I had to laugh to myself. Hell, she gave vanity a whole new definition.

I was surprised to see the black girl as I exited Tonya's office. She was hanging out in the hallway.

'What are you so happy about, James?' said Alley.

'I'm alive and well at Telegraph, baby!'

DINNER

I felt good as I sat down to dinner. I'd had a pretty good day. I talked to everyone, even the black girl. She was even kind of cute. After dinner I emailed all my new Asian gals and asked a couple of them to meet me for coffee the next morning. I made one date for 11 a.m. at the academic bookstore and one later on at the Western Café, a small place right down the street from the bookstore.

At the final group meeting that night I met an old guy I hadn't seen before. He had a bad ulcer and had just come back from treatment at Triumph General. Mary asked me to introduce myself.

'Hello, I'm James,' I said.

'One two three four five six seven eight nine ten: I'm Amos, nice to meet you.'

Amos told me he always had to count to ten before saying hello to a new person. He was slowly getting over that problem, but he had other issues too. I immediately liked Amos, even though he talked a mile a minute – like Barney, only with more charm.

'One two three four: you know, James, I couldn't walk or talk the first six weeks I was here.' Before I could respond he said, 'One two three four: you know, James, I couldn't walk or talk the first six weeks I was here.'

'Oh yeah?' I said.

'One two three four five six: you act like you don't believe me, James!'

'Yes, I believe you, Barney.'

'One two three four five: James doesn't believe I couldn't walk or talk when I first got here, Mary, so tell him!' said Amos.

'I didn't say I didn't believe him, Mary.'

Mary said that she wasn't here when Amos had first arrived but she'd heard that he'd had trouble talking and walking.

'See, James, I told you!'

I started to say something but what was the use? I might have believed he couldn't walk, but not talking – the way he rambled on – that was too hard to believe. It struck me that I'd called him Barney. Hey, if you closed your eyes . . .

Poor Teddy was shaking again. His day was a one and his anxiety was a ten. I noticed he'd begun to show anger when he reported his scores. When they asked if anybody had feedback for him, I spoke up. 'I think he needs to talk to the Doctor about trying something else for his anxiety. I don't think anybody can get cured if they're this anxious and depressed.'

The counsellor said that was good feedback. I knew from knowing Teddy Bear a short time that he wouldn't do anything about it. I would mention it to the Doc myself.

My turn to speak finally came round and I said my day was an eight and my anxiety a four. I was just about to jump up, as class was over, when Barney spouted off.

'We didn't give James any feedback.'

I told everyone my day was so good because I met a cute Japanese girl. Bragging, of course, to make up for my insecurities.

THE SOCIAL WORKER

I got up the next morning and was told I was to go over to building B and meet with Jimmy, my social worker. Funny, I didn't know I had a social worker. His office was next to Tonya's and I wasn't in the mood to see her so I took off my shoes and tiptoed by her room and into Jimmy's. Jimmy was a stocky little man.

'You look a little spaced out,' he said. 'Didn't you get any sleep?'

Oh no! Tonya had told him, too. I told myself not to panic. But my OCD kicked in. 'Did Tonya tell you about my problem?'

'What problem?'

Now I started to freak again. Anxiety was shooting through my veins.

'Hey, I didn't mean to freak you out. I was just giving you some exposure,' said Jimmy.

I was relieved, yet angry with myself for giving in. Jimmy told me he heard I was making progress, more than most in their first couple of weeks. I then asked Jimmy how long a person could stay here.

'Usually two to three months.'

I asked him what if Tonya said I was ready to go but I really wasn't. Jimmy asked me if it was my OCD causing me to keep asking about that. The truth was I was having a ball here: great food, cute counsellors, basketball and all my cute Asian girls from Telegraph. Not to mention I was getting better!

'Yeah, Jimmy, OCD.'

RAY RAY

I caught the bus to Telegraph Avenue, determined this time to enter People's Park. I'd been putting it off because I'd heard it had been a no-go area for the police in the past because all the junkies, dealers and other criminals thought the place belonged to them. The university had it under control again now, and I think it was meant to be much more respectable, and even nice, but it still maintained its reputation for being radical. I'd also been putting it off because I'd been having so much fun on Telegraph, of course.

That thing with the social worker was really going round in my head. Why hadn't I been able to ride out his deliberate jibe about being spaced out? It seemed every time I got a little confidence, something like that would shut me down. I needed to try harder, and going to the Park brandishing a *High Times* would be a big step in the right direction.

Of course, that didn't stop me from meeting a French girl on the bus. She was an au pair and beautiful. I did the usual and got her email address. I said to her, '*Parlez-vous Français?*' as I walked up to the front of the bus. I jumped out at the next stop, hoping she wouldn't know that every schmuck in America knew those three words.

I proceeded to the news-stand on Telegraph Avenue to pick up the *High Times*. I entered the store and nervously walked around, trying to build up my courage. It was easy to find because the cover was basically just an image of a giant marijuana plant. I quickly picked it up and paid for it. As soon as I walked outside, I ripped the plastic cover off so I could rub my hands across the pictures. I was surprised to find out that I had virtually no anxiety. Wow, unbelievable, I was thinking.

I walked the half-block to the Park entrance and strolled in, feeling fairly confident. It did turn out to be nice, with lots of open spaces softly carpeted with thriving, well-kept grass. After wandering around for a bit, I chanced across Jazz and Rage standing in a small group. They were talking to a couple of punks I had never seen before. One of them was older and covered with tattoos. He had an air of danger about him that separated him from the pack. The other guy was tall and well built and carried a large, green briefcase. I had an ominous feeling about those two.

Jazz spotted me and hurried over towards me. I quickly panicked and rolled the magazine up and stuck it in my back pocket. Jazz asked me if I could donate to a bottle of vodka. I told him I'd bummed a dollar earlier and gave it to him. Within seconds he was on his way. I liked this guy. He was an alcoholic and a drug addict, but he had a funny personality. He would yell out at the straight people, 'You got any money for a lowlife drug addict? I'll leave town for five bucks!' He grew up in South Carolina and had a broken home and the whole sad story. I had despised people like Jazz and Rage before and stayed completely away from them. Now I actually enjoyed their company.

Jazz got back and luckily, by then, the scary-looking pair had departed. I hung out with Jazz and Rage for about an hour, watching them drink their vodka. I had to refuse when they offered me some, as Within Reach didn't allow drinking, but luckily they just saw it as all the more for them. I eventually headed back to Telegraph to get myself a Dr Pepper: a far cry from vodka, but a drink that had become totemic for me. Many years ago in Hollywood, when I was a starving actor, I found I could somehow make it through the day if I had a Dr Pepper. That was my one constant in glamorous Hollywood. Of course, when I rounded up a little money, I would live high on the hog: I would get a Snickers bar and a *USA Today*.

'Hey, buddy. It's not raining, you're just hallucinating!'

I snapped out of my daydream and froze like an ice cube. Where was this coming from? I quickly looked around and spotted this old hippy leaning on a shopping cart just outside the news-stand. He looked like he'd just come out of

Woodstock! Dirty, long hair, unkempt beard, sandals, beads: the total package. I quickly walked over to him, looking for some reassurance. Just as I was going to speak, he went off on a crazy ramble.

'Hey, dude, Kenny here. Give me some money or give me a job but I would prefer the money. I was world champion surfer on the big island!'

'Sir, why did you ask me about hallucinating?' I said.

'Why, are you tripping, dude?' he said.

Another full-frontal anxiety attack was building! I quickly said this, hoping it might diffuse it: 'Do I look like I'm tripping, sir?'

'Everybody looks like they're tripping to me, dude!'

'So you weren't talking about me specifically, sir?'

He didn't answer my question and went off on another monologue. He was right up there with Barney, Amos and Anna. Hell, he was probably taking stimulants too!

'Can you give me a fucking job man as that would be far fucking out if you could but I want fifty cents more an hour than the Mexicans at your landscaping business and you know I was world champion surfer in Hawaii and I'm a health nut, man, look at my arms!'

He stuck his skinny arms towards me and I quickly backed away. 'I only eat natural things. I don't do drugs no more either,' he said.

I started to relax a bit as he said the magic words: 'I don't do drugs.'

A bit calmer now, I tried to remember if I had met this guy before and told him about a landscaping job. Hell, no, I thought. A guy like this I would remember!

'Sir, why do you think I have a job for you?' I said.

'Anyone who calls me "sir" has to own his own business,' he said.

He was right. I used the 'sir' word with anyone when I was anxious. A moment later I found myself looking in his shopping cart. I assume I was trying to get my mind onto another subject. I spotted a half-full glass bottle of orange juice. I thought this would be the ultimate exposure. If I could drink after him, then the sky was the limit! Though, granted, he had said he'd quit drugs.

I breathed slowly and tried to gain some confidence.

'Hey, dude,' I finally said, 'can I have a drink of your orange juice?'

'I don't drink after no one, man!'

That shocked me. He must have been the only homeless guy in the entire universe who didn't drink after anybody.

I was thinking of my next move when he darted over to a guy walking out of a bistro holding a sandwich and asked for part of it. The college student, in shock, gave him the rest of his half-eaten sandwich. Kenny ate it like a dog that hadn't eaten for weeks. I guess eating after someone was OK in Kenny's mind.

I decided I would never get total reassurance from Kenny and prodding him about anything would just make it worse. I also knew I'd had enough of him and was about to make my exit when he popped up in front of me and said, 'Hey, dude, you got any 'erb to smoke?'

The anxiety came rushing back. 'You just told me you quit drugs!' I said.

''Erb is not a drug, dude. It's natural. It's just a herb. Did you know Moses smoked 'erb, man? He had to, to put up with all those dudes tripping out in the desert!'

I just stood back and gasped. I had never met anybody like him.

He took a quick pause then started up again. 'If I don't get a job soon, man, I'm hitchhiking back to Hawaii.'

It took me a moment to digest this. I finally gathered my thoughts and said this to him: 'You can't hitchhike to Hawaii, man.'

'Why?' he said.

'Because there's a big fat ocean standing in your way!'

'You never heard of Moses parting the red fricking sea, man?'

I nodded and said, 'What's that got to do with you?'

He looked around the Avenue for a moment before whispering in my ear: 'You're looking at him, dude.'

I was lost for words, and in my case that was very unusual. How crazy must I have been to need reassurance from him? I started feeling good about not drinking after him. On the flip-side of that, if I could drink or eat something after him, I would be cured. I was not up to that task just yet. I gave him a dollar and headed out across the street when I heard his loud, resonating voice one more time.

'Hey, dude, still doing 'erb at your age!'

I turned and saw the *High Times* sticking out of my pocket. I had to laugh, as only a burnt-out hippy would have noticed that. I came to the realisation that I did have one thing in common with Kenny: we were both full of shit!

I was a bit dazed and confused as I made my way along the Avenue, heading back to the Park. I spotted another homeless man and handed him a dollar – not for exposure, but because I'd been doing that all my life. I somehow thought that God would say, 'James is a piece of shit BUT he always helped the homeless.' Of course, in the grand scheme of things that wouldn't count for much, but hey . . .

I started thinking about what one of the therapists had said earlier that morning as I walked down the street: go towards your anxiety instead of away from it. I took that to mean keep doing things that cause you anxiety. I started touching trash can after trash can. I finally stopped when I saw a newspaper sticking out of one. Although anxious, I managed to take it out and read it.

A moment later I felt a tap on my back. I was terrified to turn around because Kenny might have followed me.

'Where have you been, James? I look all over for you.'

I turned around and, to my delight, it was Ray Ray. She had her hair up and looked beautiful. I asked her to go for coffee with me. She excitedly said yes. I realised she was only 19 and I was at least twice her age, but, that said, I was thrilled this beautiful, unassuming girl had been looking for me. I invited her to come to the house that night and visit. She thought about it and said, 'Do I get to meet the rest of the research team?'

I had to keep from laughing as we went and had coffee.

An hour later we started walking to the bus stop and, as usual, my guilt kicked in. Yes, I'd had that conversation with Kenny, which he'd initiated, but afterwards I should have gone back to the Park to walk around the punks exposing my *High Times* magazine. Instead, I was hanging out with Ray Ray. Impulsively I grabbed her hand and headed back up the Avenue.

I didn't really know what I was doing, but I suppose I wanted to talk to some homeless people. For some reason, though, all the homeless on Telegraph seemed to have disappeared. We ended up just walking around until something at a store window caught my attention. It was a pipe shop and the display case was lined with bongs and other drug paraphernalia. I wanted to go in but was terrified.

'Are you mad, James, because I interfere with research today?' said my sweet Ray Ray. That was the kick in the ass

I needed. I quickly entered, with Ray Ray in tow. The place was a hippy's dream. Bongs and pipes of all shapes and sizes. It wasn't long before I spotted the ultimate exposure: a pack of Ecstasy cigarettes.

The cashier came over and asked if he could help me. I pointed at a pack and said, 'Do they have real, uh . . .?'

'Excuse me?' he said.

'I'll take a pack of those.'

I was too much of a coward even to say the word and here I was hoping to smoke one. Ray Ray didn't help my anxiety either when she said to me, 'James, I have bong too.'

I paid for the smokes and nervously walked out of the store. I kept repeating this in my mind: 'Go towards your anxiety instead of away from it.' I quickly opened the pack and stuck one in my mouth.

Fate was against me again because two of the punks from the Park popped up out of nowhere. I figured I should quickly say something before they noticed what type of cigarettes I was smoking. 'Hey, where's Rage and Jazz and does anyone got a light?'

They told me that Rage and Jazz had gone to score some vodka before one of the punks pulled out a lighter and said, 'Hey, man, Ex. Give me one. I get a real buzz from them!'

My anxiety was up and running. He quickly grabbed one from the pack and lit both of us up. I took a big puff and felt nothing special.

'You're full of shit, man, because those things suck!' said the other one.

He'd unknowingly given me some temporary relief. It was fifty-fifty and I decided to bail before someone broke the tie. I grabbed Ray Ray and took off for the terminal. 'Hey, James, I want smoke one,' said Ray Ray.

'No,' I said. 'That would be giving me reassurance.'

'What resurance mean, James?'

I told her it meant nothing and that the Ex cigarettes tasted terrible. I quickly threw them away. I felt good about my exposures now and could relax on the way home.

Ray Ray began to open up to me a bit on the bus. She told me she had a job as a nanny but she didn't like the family because they gave her a curfew and she didn't like having to come home so early on her nights out. She was from a small town in Mexico and wanted to travel around. She told me she was a pothead and smoked any time she could get some. It was surreal to me how I was so involved with the drug culture now. She also told me she'd met a man who'd offered her a job and a place to stay, as he was worried about her.

I told her this: 'Every man wants to protect every woman from everyone but himself!'

She smiled at me but I was serious.

When we got to my stop, I told her to wait at the doughnut shop because I had some work to complete with my group and that I would be back for her shortly.

I went to group in a good mood. I told everybody my day was a nine because I'd met a beautiful girl. Most of my fellow patients, like Barney, Amos and Lisa, said they were happy I was doing well etc. I didn't reciprocate, as usual.

I was just about to get up and go after Ray Ray when Barney popped off. 'James, how come you never give any of us fellow patients feedback? We always tell you to hang in there and try harder and things will get better. We say positive things to you every day and we get nothing from you!'

Barney was right. I gave feedback only once, for Teddy Bear.

'Because I don't think any of you mean what you say. It's just words: no feelings behind them,' I said.

I angrily ran into the other room.

A moment later Lisa came up. 'James, we mean the best for you. That is the only reason we give you feedback. Even Barney.'

I felt a knot in my stomach. I'd let this sweet girl down when I wouldn't touch her chair and here she was worrying about me. I smiled at Lisa and headed for the front door to go and get Ray Ray. Of course Lisa was right. Why had I said what I'd just said? My conclusion: I was afraid to get attached to anyone. A sure way to accomplish that: be rude and withdrawn. Unfortunately for me, mission accomplished.

THE GAME

As we walked up the hill, Ray Ray noticed the big Triumph sign.

'James, you living in hospital?'

Again, years of lying meant that I always had another one up my sleeve, ready to brandish. 'No, it's just a short cut to the research centre.'

I figured I could pull this off for three reasons: first, Ray Ray was Mexican and spoke so-so English; second, all the patients were drugged up to varying degrees; third, due to their illnesses, most patients had the personality of a rock, and thus they would steer clear of Ray Ray.

We entered the house and walked into the living room. The big guy and Amos stared at Ray Ray like they'd never seen a beautiful girl; at least, not a real one. I started to introduce them but they scurried off into another room, terrified. My subconscious plan was to show Dorwina and the other counsellors that I had a babe; and she was just as good, or better, than any of them.

I heard noises in the game room and was just about to

enter when Amos popped back in the room and started up on some new obsession of his.

'James, guess what? I started working as a volunteer at the Homeward Manor nursing home the best in Berkeley and the supervisor Miss Davis says I'm the best they ever had. It's top notch!'

'Well, that's good. Amos, this is . . .'

'James, guess what? I started working as a volunteer at the Homeward Manor nursing home the best in Berkeley and the supervisor Miss Davis says I'm the best they ever had! It's top notch, the best in Berkeley! James, guess what? I started working . . .'

I quickly grabbed Ray Ray and took her into the computer room.

'James, why does that man keep repeating himself?' said Ray Ray.

I pondered a moment. 'I told him this morning you were from Mexico and he's trying to help you improve your English.'

'He's a very kind man, James.'

A moment later Amos entered the computer room.

'James, I started a new job at the Homeward Manor nursing home and . . .'

Ray Ray impulsively grabbed frail little Amos, picked him up and laid a big kiss on him!

Amos ran out of the room like a scalded cat. Like I said before, most of the patients here, including me, had never had any relationships because of their disorders, and Amos was no exception. He was a 65-year-old bachelor. The good news was he hadn't counted to ten before saying hello.

I grabbed Ray Ray's hand and entered the game room. Dorwina and a part-time counsellor named Annie were sitting at the table playing a game.

'We want to play,' I said.

You could have heard a pin drop. Dorwina and Annie stared at this awesome creature standing beside me. All of their insecurities were exposed as the beautiful Ray Ray towered over them. I knew she was driving them crazy but I needed even more.

'This is Ray Ray, my new girlfriend.'

Their mouths dropped! Man, was I digging it. I found Ray Ray a chair and we joined the game. Ray Ray and I were together on a team. In the game, you had to pick a card that had a letter of the alphabet and a type of object on it. For example, you might have to describe a car that starts with the letter A. Annie said the most creative answers were the best – you'd even get an extra point for a real exotic answer.

I had to help Ray Ray a lot because her answers tended to have a Spanish slant. We played for about an hour and ended up a point behind as we approached the last round. The last question was to name a type of dog that starts with T.

Dorwina and Annie both said 'Terrier', and I gave the same answer.

'Taco Bell!' shouted Ray Ray.

'That's not a dog,' said Dorwina.

'Yeah, the little dog on the commercials,' said Ray Ray.

'Good stuff, Ray Ray.' I clapped my hands in approval.

Dorwina shook her head in disapproval.

'You said at the beginning that creativity carries a lot of weight on being correct or not,' I said.

Dorwina suggested that we vote. Ray Ray and I said the word was good; Dorwina said no good. I thought Annie would vote no because she was just a part-time counsellor and Dorwina was top dog around here.

'I have to vote yes because that's very creative,' said Annie.

I grabbed Ray Ray and jumped up and down like we'd just won the Super Bowl. Dorwina got up sulking and walked to the other room. The nose insult and now this.

I put my arm around Ray Ray and decided to parade her one last time through the living room. Yes, I was showing off! The big guy and all the patients stared at her without speaking. They had just taken their evening meds, in that zombie-type state.

I walked Ray Ray to the bus stop and kissed her goodbye. I was feeling great.

'James,' she said. 'I have one question for you. Why do all the researchers look so tired?'

HELL TO PAY

The morning alarm woke me up. I'd noticed that the guy from Philly hadn't been getting up recently so I yelled at him. He just ignored me; so be it. I went down to breakfast and I noticed all of the staff looking at me differently.

Tonya showed up at breakfast and told me to meet her at ten in her office. I was puzzled. I wasn't supposed to meet her until tomorrow. Before she walked away from the table she looked straight at me and said, 'I heard you had Jennifer Lopez over here last night.'

Oh, man. I guess I knew in some way this was going to happen. I tried to figure out why I really brought the young girl over. Of course, I must have known there would be controversy. Was it to prove my manhood; that I could still pick up women? But why bring her here? No one in their right mind would do that, especially after I'd been warned that I would have to go home if I couldn't control this. Maybe I was showing off to the other patients: I could do something they could never do. Of course, there was the sabotage thing also. I wasn't worthy to get better and have a decent life. I believed I was a bad person and should be kicked out.

I went to Tonya's office expecting the worst. Tonya reminded me why I was here and remarked that my date was a very young woman. Then she hit me with something unexpected.

'It says here on your form sheet that you answered four days in a row that your day was a ten because you met an attractive woman.'

I didn't remember giving tens – maybe nines – but either way she had me. 'Yes, but I met those girls on the bus, not during my exposure time. And you know, Tonya, it's good exposure for me to walk up to strangers and chat with them without asking for reassurance.'

'Why not walk up to strange men, then?' she said.

She had me on that one.

'The problem with that is the men will think I'm gay and hitting on them,' I said. I pulled that one out of my butt!

'Be straight with me, James. You must have some idea why you're so obsessed with all these women.'

'I thought we already talked about this.'

'We touched on it,' said Tonya.

'It's like I'm on this quest to find the perfect woman. Maybe to make up for my mother. That's why I go for woman after woman. Whenever I meet someone who seems so real to me and right for me, I say something to scare her off. Or I will look for a flaw until I find one.'

'You're doomed to fail, James. You meet a woman and search for flaws. Of course, sooner or later, even seemingly

80

the most perfect girl has flaws. We all have flaws. That's part of being human.'

Of course, I knew she was right. I am not a good person and don't deserve a nice person so I sabotage any possible chance. My one hope was that some girl would see through my ruse and know I don't mean the things I say or do. I had been sabotaging any possible relationship even before I got sick.

Tonya's next request threw me for another loop: 'So, tell me more about your mother.'

'Well, like I said, she gave me up. That kind of says it all.'

'How about your dad?' said Tonya.

'Well, Tonya, let me describe my dad in this way. He wanted me to catch the bus here all the way from Louisiana, even in my bad shape, to save paying the plane fare. That's the kind of guy he is. I remember when I was a kid of about 13 and he had married my newest stepmother, a gal of about 20. Now, we're talking early '60s in small-town Kansas. I remember a kid I used to play with told me his mother wouldn't let him come over any more because we weren't the right kind of people. That's crushing for a kid! My dad never cared for me, or my brother. He only cared for women and money. Still does. I'd get passed around from relative to relative depending on who could afford to keep me, not on who I wanted to stay with, because he never supported me financially or emotionally as a child. Even now he charges my brother money just for doing odd jobs at my brother's car lot, like changing the light bulbs.

'I moved to Louisiana to live with my mother when I was 13. At least she tried to make up for it. She gave me all the money she could scrape up. Of course, I hated her more for that. I wish she had told me to get out and earn my own money. I hated myself for taking her money.

'The last time I saw my dad he was waking me up at four in the morning to buy me breakfast.'

'What's wrong with that?' said Tonya.

'I asked for milk when I ordered and he told me milk doesn't come with the 99-cent special! I told the bastard not to wake me up at four in the morning again and walked out.'

Tonya asked me if that was a true story.

'Why do you ask that?' I said.

'You told me you're a bit of a con man.'

'Well, it might have been my uncle instead.'

Tonya gave me a mischievous smile. It was obvious that she was overjoyed that I had broken down and told her intimate details about my life. I guess Tonya figured I was very vulnerable now, so why not keep it going.

'James, do you love your mother and father?'

'Like I said before, I'm incapable of love. No one has ever loved me, either. I came into this world alone and I'll die alone.'

'That's sad, James.'

'You got to go with the hand that was dealt you, Tonya.'

'No, you don't, James. You can change.'

'I'm tired, Tonya. Can we call it a day?'

'OK, James, if that's what you want. But you have to keep this woman thing under control, comprende?'

'Comprende,' I said, smiling.

I was wasted and wanted to go back to Within Reach. I reached for the doorknob and was exiting when I heard this: 'I'm glad you opened up to me today,' said Tonya.

I nodded.

'James, did the girl from last night know you are a patient here?'

I don't know if I wanted to be honest or brag about the fact that I'd pulled it off. 'I told her we are all doing research on homeless people together and Within Reach is the centre where we turn in all our data; and that, in order to develop a deeper bond, we share living quarters here.'

Tonya just shook her head. 'Goodbye, James.'

I smiled and walked out of the room. I was surprised to see Alley hanging outside by the door again. I figured maybe she was Tonya's next appointment so I waved and continued on my way. Maybe I was wrong about Tonya. She genuinely seemed concerned about me.

PO' WHITE TRASH

My confidence was way up so I quickly set off for Telegraph and the People's Park to do some exposures with my *High Times* in full view. I wandered all around the area but my freaks were nowhere to be found. I quickly realised that the object of their existence was to get high: that was why I couldn't find anybody. They were out there in the jungle somewhere looking for the pill or needle or whatever to get that buzz. It was sad.

I was just about to leave when I spotted a couple of punks entering the Park. Here was my chance. I hurried in after them, soon located them and sat right across from them. I opened my magazine wide and started singing to draw their attention. A few minutes later I had company. One of the punks came over and said, 'Hey, dude, you want to buy some 'erb?'

I was more anxious than I thought I'd be. I was grasping for the right words when he continued. 'I saw you looking at your magazine so I figured you were a fellow toker. I got that issue too.'

'I'm flat busted, man, but I'll look you up when I get a little bread together,' I said.

The punk smiled and told me he was around the Park a lot and to come and find him when I had some jingle. He went back to his buddy and a few moments later they disappeared. I hung around for a while but there was no more action. Even Kenny was nowhere to be found. I told myself I had no choice but to throw in the towel and go to the academic bookstore.

I met four girls there, got their email addresses and worked my way back to the bus stop. I stood at the stop until I spotted another beautiful Asian girl on the other side of the road. I tried not to go after her but I couldn't stop myself. The bus I needed had even pulled up, but I figured she was worth being late for. I found her and ended up collecting another email address. Luckily, my bus was still boarding just as I returned.

I made my way back to the house and Alley greeted me at the door. 'Come on, James, we've got a new patient coming in.'

'Yeah,' I said.

'Maybe you'll get lucky, James, and she will be an Asian girl.'

'How do you know about that? You're not in my group.'

'Come on, James. Everybody knows about that.'

Of course, my bragging about it didn't help much.

'So how's it going with Tonya?' said Alley.

'I thought she didn't like me but today she seemed so concerned about me.'

'How so?' said Alley.

'Well, she . . . hey, it's none of your business!'

I got up fast and walked into the living room. Undaunted, Alley followed me and sat right next to me.

'I'm trying to be your friend, if you'll let me,' said Alley.

'OK, friend, why did you stand up for me at lunch that day that everyone attacked me?'

'Why not?' said Alley.

'Maybe you did it because no one likes me around here?'

'Maybe.'

Alley had me confused. 'Seriously, why are you nice to me?' I said.

'I try and be nice to everyone.'

Just then Mary stood up and said a new patient would be arriving any minute. A moment later there was a loud knock on the door.

'I'll get it, Mary, because I want to welcome the new patient first.'

I winked at Alley as I made my way to the door. I heard some commotion going on outside as I got closer to the front door. I opened it and all I saw were teeth! Huge, yellow buckteeth. I backed away from the door and this skinny little barefoot guy entered with his family.

'I'm Jerry, the new patient, and this is my family.'

The first thing that entered my mind was that they looked like those people from that movie *Deliverance*. The other, and most important, thing that entered my mind: the new patient was not female.

No one was ready for what happened next. Without warning they all turned around and walked out the front door. A brief scuffle was heard but it was hard to make out what they were fighting about. A moment later we clearly heard this: 'I want to stay this time!'

All of us patients stood around grinning.

A moment later Jerry entered like nothing had happened and said, 'I'm Jerry, the new patient. What time is dinner?'

Things had just been starting to get better at Within Reach, but I had a gut feeling that this character was going to put a crick in it. The counsellors introduced him to the group and asked if he would like to get up and tell us something about himself. I could hardly wait to hear his story. I also noticed that he didn't have a suitcase. That would account somewhat for the yellow teeth.

He got up and said, 'I'm from New York City. I have five kids. My girlfriend left me because of my OCD. I have problems with tying my shoes. I tie them hundreds of times before I feel they're right. I comb my hair hundreds of times before I feel right. I got kicked out of my trailer park because I could never make it on time to pay my rent because of my OCD.'

One of the counsellors asked if we had any questions we would like to ask him. I started whispering to Alley, 'Why can't your OCD be brushing your teeth too much?'

'James, are you asking Jerry a question?' said Mary.

'No, I just wanted to welcome him here.'

'That's nice of you, James. Maybe we can learn some things about New York City from Jerry. OK, let's break for dinner,' said Mary.

As we got up to go to the dining room, I leaned over to Alley and said, 'I did learn something from Terry.'

'Jerry. And what might that be?' said Alley.

'They got poooooooooooooo' white trash in New York City too! I thought it only existed in the south, where I'm from.'

Alley told me I was being too hard on the guy. Of course, she was right. Truth was I was no stranger to living in trailers, and I hadn't even had running water in one for five years. If anyone was po' white trash, I was. I somehow had deluded myself that I didn't fit that category.

I entered the dining room and spotted Po' White. He was sitting alone. I decided to make up for my premature judgment of him and went over and sat next to him. 'There's a good ball game on tonight. I was thinking maybe we could watch it together,' I said.

'I hate sports,' he said.

I must admit I was taken aback by his response.

'They say never trust a guy who doesn't like sports,' I said. There was a long pause. I was beginning to feel real uncomfortable. I decided to try another tack. 'You know, I'm a small-time actor and have a movie out on PBS. It's a cute comedy.'

'I only like action movies,' he said.

My blood was boiling over. I was just about to explode and go off on Po' White when Alley came to the rescue.

'Get some dessert, James,' said Alley.

A moment later Dorwina yelled out, 'If anybody wants to go rent a video, I'm going to the store.'

'I do!' said Po' White. He immediately ran out the door.

'What happened?' said Alley. 'I could see your anger from across the table.'

'Pooooooooooooooooooooooooooooo' white trash!' I yelled out.

Even supersensitive Alley had to laugh at that. I'd tried to be nice and it had backfired. He had five kids, had never married and had no qualms about wasting money on movies. Yes, indeed, there was po' white trash in New York City!

THE OUTING

I found out that we all had to go on an outing this night, I guess on the premise that it would help us to bond together. I didn't really want to go but I had no choice. I quickly ran to an empty row of seats at the back of the van when they opened the door for us. I was hoping that I'd get to sit by myself. I got lucky when Anna sat up front with Barney. I was as happy as can be when Alley took a seat on its own in front of me.

'Hey, Dorwina, Tim and Jerry don't want to go,' said Mary.

'They have to go unless their BT gave them permission not to,' said Dorwina.

I started to panic. I tapped Alley on the shoulder and said, 'Who are Tim and Jerry?'

Alley smirked. 'You never can remember people's names, can you, James? Well, they're two fellow patients.'

'Duh. I know that!'

Alley was grinning from ear to ear for some reason. I soon found out why. Po' White and the big guy entered the van. 'Oh, shit! Please change seats with me, Alley.'

'Why?' she said.

I told her I did not want to sit by them.

'So you want me to?' she said.

'You guys go sit next to James,' said Dorwina.

Alley broke into laughter. A moment later they were right next to me.

'Excuse me, James, I just farted,' said the big guy.

'It's so nice of you to share that with me,' I said.

'Hey, Tim, you see the way Mary looks at me? Yeah, she was all over me the day I arrived,' said Po' White.

'Pleaaaaase!' I said.

'What was that?' said Po' White.

I just shook my head.

I could see Alley peeking through her seat, eating up my discomfort.

'You know, Jerry, Alley was looking at you that way too,' I said.

'Who's that?' said Po' White.

I pointed at Alley and said, 'The girl peeking through the seat!'

Alley quickly turned around.

88

'I got a crush on Dorwina,' said the big fat guy.

'Yeah, we can double date,' said Po' White.

I tried to bite my tongue but when the big guy said, 'You think Dorwina likes me, James?' it was too much.

'Listen, those girls would never go out with you two clowns!'

'You're just jealous, James,' said Po' White.

'Jealous of you? Why don't you . . .'

'James, quit joking around,' said Alley.

Alley came to my rescue again. I needed to control myself if I wanted to stay. I kept my mouth shut the rest of the way. When we filed out of the van, I literally ran away from the group and headed for the mall entrance.

'Make sure you're back by nine, James!' yelled Dorwina.

'I'll think about it,' I said.

TROUBLE IN PARADISE

I made it back to the van just on time that night. The next day I got up and headed back to Telegraph. I couldn't remember ever looking forward to getting up in the morning until I came here. I was not only getting better, but I was meeting beautiful Asian women every day. This was a paradise.

I met another Chinese girl waiting on the bus at the doughnut shop. She was a violin player. I told her that was my favourite instrument and I'd dreamed of playing until a childhood injury had ended my dreams. There was some truth in that: I did enjoy the violin whenever I chanced to hear it on the radio once in a blue moon.

I don't know what exactly precipitated my behaviour that evening when I got back to the house, but I found myself

smarting off to all the counsellors. It started when I had to
go to the bathroom but someone was in there. Sharing one
bathroom with so many people was bad enough, but half of
them would stay in there forever, it seemed, ritualising. They
would be flushing the toilet a hundred times just to make
sure they'd done it, or wiping their asses a hundred times
just to make sure they were clean. Now a lot of us in the
house didn't have those particular obsessions but we had to
pay the consequences and stand around trying not to pee in
our pants, or worse, if you know what I mean.

I finally went up to Dorwina and told her I had to pee and
couldn't wait. I asked her to open up an upstairs bathroom.
She told me to hold on, and that she would find out who was
in the restroom and hurry them up. Of course, I'd popped off
to her in front of everybody at the outing so I wasn't exactly
in her good books. I was feeling impatient.

'You can't even go to the bathroom in this place! I'm tired
of you people telling me what to do and I don't care if you
write me up!'

Truth was, I didn't really have to go that bad but, for some
unknown reason, I was making a scene. I also told Mary that
I needed some ibuprofen for my leg because I'd hurt it
jogging to the bus stop that morning. I watched as she went
through the medicine kit and I spotted a bottle of Advil. I
pointed it out to her.

'You said ibuprofen,' she said.

I told her that Advil was ibuprofen. She said it wasn't.

Now, Mary was the nicest counsellor here but she did
seem a little blonde, let's say. I blurted out, 'Look on the
ingredients, you scatterbrained goof!'

I finally got one of the other counsellors to agree with me on
the Advil: not to make Mary look bad but to give me
reassurance. I'm sure, unless you have had anxiety attacks,

you would have thought I was trying to show you up. Unfortunately for me, that's what Mary thought.

The next couple of days I carried on smarting off to all the counsellors. I had no reason to but I did. I got up a few mornings later and prepared for my usual weekly meeting with Dr Swenson. I ate breakfast and walked into the waiting room. A moment later Jimmy the social worker showed up. I asked him what he was up to and he said I should know why he was here. I feigned surprise, even though I knew it was to do with my behaviour towards the counsellors. A moment later the Doc opened his door and invited us in. He looked at me a moment then opened up.

'James, I hear you're being a smart ass with the counsellors and picking on some of the other patients.'

I responded, 'These girls are ganging up on me!'

The Doc waited a moment. 'I haven't heard any complaints from the male counsellors, so I suspect you have a lot of anger towards women.'

'I love broads. I'm obsessed with them, as I told you before.'

'A man obsessed with women doesn't go around calling them broads,' said the Doc.

I began to panic. 'Does this mean I'm going to be kicked out?'

Jimmy responded, 'We don't want you to get kicked out. That's why we're having this meeting.'

My anxiety shot straight to the top. What would I do if I got kicked out? This place was my only hope. I was desperate. I started telling the Doc everything.

'Doc, I always sabotage anything good. I know this place can help me, but my low self-esteem tells me I don't deserve to get well because I'm a terrible person and I deserve the worst.'

Now, to be honest I don't know if I was totally sincere or trying to con the Doc so he wouldn't kick me out. But why else would I get myself in these predicaments, especially when things were going great?

I finally said, 'Doc, you're not going to kick me out, are you?'

The Doc laughed. 'Oh, we don't kick anybody out unless they threaten to beat me up!'

He had kind of a nervous laugh. I tried to laugh with him. I looked over at Jimmy, trying to include him in the laughter. His face was as serious as Mt Rushmore. A moment later he got up and excused himself. I decided I would get him back that night at basketball. The Doc said to relax and we would focus on our weekly meeting.

'So, I hear you had some young honey over here the other night.'

'We're allowed to have company, as you well know.'

'So, what's an old fart like you doing with a young girl like that?'

I didn't really know what to say. Truth was I was probably showing off to the counsellors and the other patients that I was such a ladies' man.

'I thought we decided it wasn't in your best interest to be concentrating on women while you're here.'

I told him I'd met the girl on my free time, which was a lie. He also said the counsellors had noticed me on the Internet emailing a lot of women. Of course I denied that and said they were girls I had met before coming here. He suggested I stay off the Net. I refused and told him I had close friends who tended to cheer me up with emails: another lie. I told him Dorwina hated me because I'd showed her up and she'd got the other girls to hate me too.

The Doc responded calmly: 'What about Mary? She told

me you give her a hard time all the time. I'll tell you this: Mary is the easiest going girl on the staff and if you can't get along with her, well . . .'

'Mary doesn't like me because I called her a space cadet. I mean, she is a scatterbrain!'

The Doctor just smiled. He knew that I knew that I was the one causing problems, not the counsellors. He told me to look at this as a challenge: that to be friends with Mary and the other female counsellors was a way to practise getting along with women. I knew that Mary was a sweet girl and had my best interests at heart. He said that all the counsellors had my best interests at heart. Now, I wasn't buying that at all. Call me paranoid, but I knew Dorwina would have a party if I got kicked out!

I knew I had just a few minutes of session time left so I threw this at the Doc: 'Doc, I feel like the guy who went to a movie a few days after attending the funeral of a close relative. He found himself crying his eyes out at the movie and told everyone how sad and depressed it made him and that he highly recommended seeing it because it touched him so deeply. A few weeks later a friend invites him to the same movie. This time he finds himself laughing during the movie and agrees later with his friend that the movie wasn't much. He realises now it was the funeral that affected him, not the movie. I'm always at the funeral, Doc. I want to see the movie a second time! Are you hip to what I'm saying, Doc?'

'Yeah, dude. I'm hip,' said Dr Swenson.

FIBRE

One of the bad things about taking my medication was that I was always constipated. The remedy was an industrial-strength laxative. And the problem with taking this laxative was that it made me fart all the time!

It got so bad that I would walk out of my room so as not to wake Philly up. I also realised eating all those fruits and salads didn't help any. When I let rip, it sounded like explosives were going off in my pants. I was terribly afraid that the women on my floor would hear me.

That's one reason I've never understood gays. I mean, how could any man even consider sleeping with another dirty, fart-popping man? Now, women hardly ever do that in public. I'm not sure if women do that at all. Of course, I don't think women do number twos either.

My concerns about farting only went so far, though, and I didn't think twice about deliberately letting them out right by the big guy's room. Why not let him take the blame? I'd had an odd conversation with the big guy that afternoon. I had walked up to use the computer and he'd jumped on it before me. He told me he had a crush on Jean Smith – an actress in some B movies I've never heard of, like *The Monsters from Space*, or something like that – and he had tracked down her phone number in Texas and called her. He said that, when he left here, he was going to move to North Carolina, where she was filming some show. I asked him what he'd said when she'd answered the phone. He said he'd just hung up. I felt sorry for the big guy for the first time. His fantasies were all he had. I knew and he knew that he would never meet this girl.

I cut a big fart outside his room and ran back into mine. It didn't work. I heard one of the girls yell, 'There goes James again!' I panicked and called into the big guy's room, 'Hey, cut it out in there, I'm trying to sleep!'

I smiled as I closed my door. Philly was sound asleep as usual. I figured that that was the only time he felt any peace.

I was thinking about reading a book when I heard a light tap on my door. I put on my sweatshirt and jogging bottoms and went to answer it. I was surprised to see Alley.

'What's up, Alley?' I said.

She said that something was bothering her and she needed to talk to me about it.

'What I want to know, James, is how come you never look me in the face when I'm talking to you?'

'I never look anyone in the face.'

'Bullshit! I see the way you look at Mary and the other girls. And you even look Po' White Trash in the face!'

I started to make up another story but I knew Alley was too sharp for this. She looked hurt and turned away.

'What's brought this on? I thought we were kind of getting along.'

'Why, because I stood up for you when the rest attacked you?'

I'm not sure why I gave the answer I gave; maybe it was because I was attracted to Alley. 'OK, Alley. I don't look at you in the face 'cause I don't like black folk. Nobody in my family likes them. Nobody in my town likes them. Are you happy now? You can report me as a racist and get me kicked out of here.'

The room got real quiet. Boy, did I do myself in this time. Alley slowly walked out of the room. Man, was I done. I might as well have packed my bags. I knew that they would have no choice but to throw me out. I'd made so much progress and now I was toast. I felt like crying, but I couldn't. I was numb. The really sad thing was I liked Alley. I just didn't have the guts to tell her, so I took this way out. What a fool I was!

I packed my bags. I figured I would sneak out. It would be better than saying goodbye to the Doc and some of the patients. There was a security/counsellor-type guy downstairs who looked like Peter Lorre, the actor, and was somewhat fondly called Igor, because he worked the graveyard shift.

He was a bit of an oddball and was known to sneak into patients' bedrooms with a big flashlight and shine it in their faces just to see if there was any hanky-panky going on. I slowly walked to the front door and was just about to unlock it when Alley grabbed my arm.

'Where in the hell are you going? You're not leaving me here to deal with Poooooooooooo' White Trash all by myself, are you?'

I didn't know what to say.

Alley continued, 'Does sabotage ring a bell? Did I tell you they call me the House Eavesdropper around here?'

I was caught off guard. Alley was a lot more than I'd bargained for. That explained why she was always hanging around the door at Tonya's office. I knew that no matter what happened at the centre, I had made a friend.

Suddenly, there was a loud sound as the front door was shut and Igor was making his way towards the front.

'Who's there?' yelled out Igor.

Alley grabbed me and pulled me into her room. 'Put your suitcase behind my door,' whispered Alley.

She knew I would never make it back to the third floor without Igor seeing me. I pushed the suitcase behind her door. Igor must have heard something because he opened Alley's door, flashing a high beam. My heart started thumping. I knew if he saw me we would both be kicked out. As he turned to see me, a loud voice cried out from the hallway.

'My stomach! I feel terrible.'

Igor immediately turned and ran out. Alley pointed at me to make a run for it. I slowly stepped outside and saw Igor standing over Teddy Bear. I noticed Teddy smiling at me so I waved a thank you and ran upstairs to my room.

Alley quickly ran over to them and said loudly, 'What happened, Igor?'

'That's not my name!' said Igor.

Teddy quickly sat up and said, 'Hey, Igor, you like the Rangers?'

Philly awakened as I ran into the room. 'Why are you walking around with a suitcase, James? OCD?'

'Yeah, OCD.'

He nodded and turned to go back to sleep. I smiled as I lay in my bed. Alley and Teddy Bear had risked expulsion to cover me. I'd never really had any friends. Not even as a child. The ones I did have I was always using to help myself. I was trying to figure an angle for those two helping me, but I couldn't come up with anything. That night I slept well for the first time I could remember and looked forward to the next morning.

MEN'S GROUP

The next morning started with a new group called the men's group: the idea being that men had things to share that they could only share amongst each other. The guy leading the group was called Dan. He was a New Yorker of Irish descent and had shiny blue eyes and that Leprechaun thing going on. It started out very quietly. Amos must have overslept because I knew he would have had something to say. Barney was a no-show too.

When Po' White started in, I thought, here we go again. I'd heard this story every morning and every evening since he'd arrived here: how his girlfriend ran away from the trailer park with his kids when he got OCD. How all his friends were losers and only ran around with him because he bought them beer. How he didn't want to see his kids in his condition. I couldn't take much more of this. I knew he didn't give a damn about his kids because he was always spending money renting movies with two girls from my floor. He told me he got four hundred dollars from social security and I guarantee not a dime was going to his four or five kids or the woman he never married. I felt like grabbing him and throwing him into the closet. I knew it was just a matter of time before I had a major confrontation with him. I hated his guts! Of course, being totally honest, a lot of it had to do with his snub of me and my movie. That was still sticking in my craw.

I finally snapped. 'Let somebody else talk. We've all heard this sob story before.'

Of course, Po' White Trash jumped back with, 'Hey, nobody was talking, so I was just helping out Dan. Why don't you talk? You never say anything, James.'

I wasn't about to share my vulnerabilities with him – or with anybody. As far as I was aware, nobody but the Doc and my BT knew my total OCD. One thing was certain: if Po' White Trash knew my condition, he would have had a field day trying to give me an anxiety attack. I bit my tongue and waited for the group to end.

When it was over, I made a mad dash for the computer, trying to beat the fat guy and Barney to it. Luckily I did and was just starting to check my emails when I felt a tap on my shoulder. I turned around and Po' White Trash was staring at me.

'I didn't appreciate your interrupting me, James!'

'You want to go outside and settle this, Po' White Trash?'

As luck would have it, Mary walked by. 'What's up, James?' she said. I knew I was in trouble. Po' White walked away towards the living room. I stopped and pleaded with Mary that he'd started it and that I was just defending myself.

'What are you talking about, James?'

'Oh, I was just practising my acting. You know I told you I was an actor? I was wondering if you saw that movie of mine on tape.'

Mary told me to get her the tape. I had weaselled out of that one. But I knew something ominous lay ahead with Po' White Trash.

EILEEN

I thought I would get me a Dr Pepper and cool down from my run in with Po' White. I sat down by myself enjoying the privacy when a girl popped up and sat down beside me. It was the tall, attractive brunette. I told her I'd thought that she and that gay guy had moved on. She proceeded to tell me he had left but she had been here all the time but, because she had her car here, she was out a lot.

'I heard you arguing with that hillbilly. I was praying he would get kicked out,' she said. She also told me this was her third time here and she was taking a break from Stanford, another affluent school in California.

Something suddenly rang a bell. Barney had told me about a patient whose dad was a millionaire in the shipping business. He said she was always 'coming and going' and somehow always got permission to stay out after curfew. He also said that when all the other patients would be doing their exposures, she would sneak upstairs, set her alarm and sleep. She always came down just in time to report her scores. He said she would always say her exposure brought her anxiety to an eight and then back to a four. This had to be her: the infamous Eileen.

She was dressed like a Wall Street professional. She rambled, 'You know, James, I won't go to Dorwina's art class because she's not qualified to teach that. And I know more about psychology than most of these pissant counsellors. Daddy wants me to be a lawyer so I can run the business. I bought some new clothes today. I can't stand the way these people dress around here, can you?'

I didn't respond, but that didn't stop her from taking all kinds of new clothes from her shopping bags to show me. She told me she couldn't stand to wear the same clothes more than once because they somehow got contaminated as she went about her day. I think that was her excuse for using daddy's credit card to bring box loads of clothes home every night.

'Of course, I never wear the same shoes either. I don't like being predictable. Did you know that Dr Swenson has been married four times? I'm glad I don't have him as my psychiatrist. And of course his son is a drug addict who hates his dad. So how can he tell me what to do when he can't even take care of his own family?'

I'd thought she was funny until she started on the Doc. He was a great man and was helping me a lot, and he was well liked by everybody.

'Where did you get this information?'

'Oh, James, I know everything that goes on here.'

'Why, because you've been here so many times?'

She ignored my question. It hit me that the Doc's son had played basketball the other night and I'd noticed how close he and his father were.

'Listen, that's not true, Eileen. I met his son and they have a great relationship, and his son had no appearance of being a drug addict, so I don't know where you get your information.'

Eileen ignored my remarks and told me she had a date. I didn't notice any OCD in her. I figured she had been here twice before because this was kind of like a holiday resort where she could lie back and take it easy.

'What is your OCD, Eileen?'

'I pick on my toes. I think I have the ugliest feet in the world. I paint my toes for hours unless someone stops me. Listen, James, I get most of my calls on my cell but if anyone calls me on the house phone, tell them I went shopping and then met some friends for dinner.'

She was gone. I was told the only way you could stay out past curfew was to get permission from your BT. Eileen had a real easy-going BT. I knew Tonya wouldn't let me stay out unless something really important came up. I would save that for Ray Ray, or one of the 25 or so women I had met already and was emailing. The thought occurred to me that maybe if Eileen had had a stricter BT, she wouldn't have been here for the third time.

Eileen was definitely a snob and thought she was better than all the other patients. She also thought she was better than all the counsellors and the doctors, for that matter. The question was, if she felt so superior, why was she even here? Deep down, I'm sure she was as insecure as the rest of us.

THE CHRISTIAN

I hurried home excitedly from Telegraph one night. I had met a cute Asian girl at the bus stop and promised to email her immediately. I walked into the house and ran to the computer. To my dismay a new patient was on it. His name was Benny. He was an average-looking guy of about 30, with jet-black hair; the kind of guy you could walk by every day for a year and still not remember.

'You know Jesus, James?' said Benny.

I was debating what answer to give him.

'You know, James, after I leave here I'm going to my fiancée's home in Michigan. Are you saved, James?'

My thoughts drifted back to the many churches I had wandered in and out of. They always had some fat layperson with pimples in the pulpit telling you that he could have had sex with many women and partied all the time but instead he chose the path of God. In truth the only sex he was giving up was his right hand! Now you get a guy up there that looks like Brad Pitt and he's telling you that he abstains from sex, drugs and rock and roll and I might buy into it. That said, I do believe in God and I've met many Christian girls in my life who would do anything for you. Now that was true Christianity – being kind to complete strangers, especially strangers like me!

Speaking of true, I was sleeping at a picnic area near Austin in the back of an old truck when a car pulled up beside me and the driver knocked on my window. I looked up to see this man and his family staring at me. My first thought was, 'Hey, they're looking for some money.' It was an easy assumption. They were driving an old bomb, had three kids and everyone was dressed in tattered clothes.

'Merry Christmas. Here's twenty dollars. God loves you!' said the man as he reached his hand out to me.

Wow! I hadn't even realised it was Christmas.

'We drive by here all the time and see you sleeping in your truck and my family and I want you to know that someone cares about you,' said the man.

My heart was overwhelmed. I had never seen such kindness. I awkwardly told the man I didn't need the money. He made sure that I wasn't just being polite. Unlike the clueless televangelists with the cars and the mansions, he had the true spirit of God.

Benny snapped me back to reality.

'You know me and my girlfriend are both virgins, James. We're saving it for our marriage.'

'Well, good for you!' I said, holding back a chuckle.

Hey, maybe I was a bit jealous. I mean this guy had a fiancée. What the hell did I have?

'Did you meet her back home?' I said.

'I haven't met her yet,' he replied.

'Excuse me?'

'I met her on Christian chat and we will meet in person as soon as I leave here.'

I started to ask him a normal question, like, 'How do you get engaged to a girl you've never met?' But I knew he would say that Jesus put them in touch, or something like that.

'How long are you going to be on the computer, guy?' I said.

'You never answered my question about being saved, James.'

I wondered what answer would get him off the computer.

'Funny you should mention that, guy, because I was hoping to get on the computer to look up some biblical information on Moses.'

'Here, the computer is yours and maybe when you finish you can join me for some fellowship.'

Benny walked away with a big smile on his face.

In reality I was closer to God than he was. I had met Moses down in Telegraph . . .

THE WHITE BREAKDANCER

I came to meet many young hustlers hanging around People's Park but one of them stood out more than most. He was short and reminded me of one of those guys you see working the carnival circuit: rotten teeth, bad skin, cheap tattoos, etc. He would steal newspapers from behind the news-stand where I bought my *High Times* and sell them to passers-by.

That in itself was not very noteworthy. One day he showed up with this cheap-looking boom-box and placed it and a cup for tips right in the middle of the Park. A moment later he was attempting to breakdance. I say attempting because he was the worst breakdancer I have ever seen.

A small crowd gathered. It was surreal. Everyone was laughing at this buffoon but he was oblivious to it. I literally fell down in hysterics. The crowd got bigger and bigger but the tip jar remained empty. Hoping it might encourage others, I pulled myself together enough to walk up to the cup and throw a dollar in it. He smiled from ear to ear with those rotten teeth. Mercifully the tape came to an end and he put my dollar in his pocket.

'How would you describe my dancing?' he said.

'Uh, uh, uh, it was interesting,' I said.

'Thanks,' he said. 'Can you stick around for my next show?'

'Well, to be honest you've given an old man like me enough excitement for one day.'

Again he flashed those rotten teeth at me.

I heard the boom-box start up again as I headed down to the bus stop on Telegraph. It was my turn to smile from ear to ear.

MY FRIEND

I was sitting in the doughnut shop one morning waiting for the bus to Telegraph when an old truck drove up and parked in front of mc. It was a white 1990 Mazda truck, exactly like the one I lived out of in Austin, Texas.

I had become closer to that truck than I was with any human. I could talk about anything to it without fear of any reprisals. The truck was old and beaten and smoke poured out of the exhaust but it never totally broke down on me. I would drive around Austin in the middle of the night looking to help someone who was having car troubles. A man I helped one night told me I was crazy to stop and that it was dangerous and that I might get killed. I wasn't scared at all. I got a good feeling helping someone and thought God might cut me a break for my good deeds. If they killed me? They'd do me a favour.

Unfortunately, as time went on, I found myself putting two quarts of oil in daily. I had to let it go. I sold it to some drifter for twenty bucks. I stared at the truck as I handed him the keys. A moment later she was gone. Impulsively I took off after it. I ran and ran and ran until she faded away in the distance. Months later I ended up with another old clunker but I kept thinking about the truck. I found myself driving around looking for it, like I'd never really said goodbye. That shows how desperately lonely my anxiety attacks and OCD had forced me to become.

SQUIGGLES

I became more and more involved with the young homeless at People's Park every day. I was on a first-name basis with a lot of them. The only guy I felt really uncomfortable with was Squiggles. He was the guy I had spotted talking to Jazz that I'd had an ominous feeling about. I was right; he was 'The Man' around here.

He had approached me the next day with Rabbit, the big muscular guy who still carried the green briefcase, and proceeded to tell me that he ran the Park and always liked to welcome strangers. Of course, I told him I'd just hitchhiked into town and was broke. Luckily it had started raining heavily so he'd postponed the interrogation. Today was another story. The sun was shining brightly. He started off by asking me why I didn't carry a backpack since I'd supposedly just got into town.

'I lost it. Anyone seen a yellow duffel bag?' I yelled out to everyone around.

'How did you manage to lose it, man?' he said.

'I was using it for a pillow and someone stole it from right off my head!'

Squiggles broke into laughter. 'How did you manage that, man?'

'I was so stoned I don't remember.'

Squiggles fell down laughing. 'Hey, punks, this dude had his pack taken out from right under his head!'

I feigned laughter too.

'Where you from, dude?' said Squiggles.

'I'm from New Orleans.'

'You don't sound like a guy from New Orleans.'

Squiggles was right. New Orleans has a unique accent; some say as distinct as New York. I, on the other hand, had a rural Louisiana accent, which is your basic southern drawl. I panicked and quickly yelled out at a homeless guy walking by, 'Anyone seen a yellow duffel bag?'

It worked for the moment. Squiggles burst out laughing

again. I knew I couldn't keep this up and was trying to think of a way out. Fate intervened. Two boys, looking about twelve or thirteen, walked by checking out the druggies.

Squiggles quickly yelled out, 'Hey! I got some stuff to make you high all night for just twenty bucks.'

The young boys looked at each other then walked a few feet away. Squiggles told me he had some good pills to get those kids hooked. That was his MO – the younger the better. I watched as the young boys began to gather all their money together. A moment later Squiggles and Rabbit joined them.

I hated guys like Squiggles. I was pretty sure that drugs had something to do with my getting OCD. Guys like Squiggles had talked me into doing drugs even though I didn't want to. I wanted to walk up to the boys and tell them I was a cop and to get the hell out of here. I knew that if Squiggles found me out, though, I was dead. I took the coward's way out and walked over to Telegraph and the academic bookstore.

I bullshitted a couple more girls, got a Big Gulp Dr Pepper then returned to People's Park. Jazz and Rage were finishing a bottle of vodka I had contributed to. Rage remarked that one minute I was in the Park and the next I was gone.

Jazz nodded and remarked, 'Hey, he only does guest appearances in here!'

We all laughed. I had become very fond of these two. Rage looked like your worst nightmare. He was big and black with rings coming out of everywhere. I'm talking nose rings, earrings, tongue rings. You name it, he wore it. Before I came here, I wouldn't have got within a hundred feet of these guys. Now I was sitting there shooting the breeze like we were old friends. I was glad that Squiggles and the young boys were nowhere in sight.

Rage told me he was on antidepressants and tranquillisers prescribed to him by the county doc. He also told me he had given a lot away to his friends to get high and he had sold his food stamps to get drug money. Jazz told me he had liver problems. He also said he was a bisexual alcoholic who happened to be an ex heroin addict. I'm sure the 'ex' meant until he could get some money to score.

'Hey, Jimbo. Jazz tried to shoot up some vodka last night right in front of the cops!' said Rage.

'I was wondering where these new needle marks came from,' said Jazz as he looked his skinny arms over.

'Hey, Jimbo, you ever hear of anyone shooting up fucking vodka before?' said Rage.

'Well, Rage, I can't say as I have.'

'Fucking vodka, Jazz , you crazy motherfucker!' said Rage as he thumped Jazz on the head. They began slapping each other around until a hash pipe fell out of Rage's pocket.

'Could you pick that up for me, Jimbo, because my fucking back is killing me?' said Rage.

I reached down, picked it up and handed it to Rage. 'Did the police try to arrest you, Jazz ?' I said.

'Hell, no, they're afraid of catching his Aids!' said Rage.

I gave them the rest of my Big Gulp and, even though they were disappointed it was only a soft drink, they took it. I pondered taking a drink after them. I knew it wasn't a good idea, especially with that last Aids remark. I was proud of myself for picking up the pipe but taking a drink from them would put me on another plateau altogether as far as my treatment was concerned.

Just then this beautiful Japanese girl walked by with her dog. I was mesmerised. She was the most beautiful woman I had ever seen. I quickly jumped up and followed her right out of the Park and into the Western Café. I got behind her in the queue and started my spiel. 'Wow, my dog could be your dog's long-lost twin!'

Her name was Mariko and she was from Santa Barbara, and also lived in Tokyo part time. Her dad owned 30 companies from Tokyo to California. I knew she was way out of my league, but I told her I was a writer from California and blah blah blah. I pulled out a wad of money to pay for her lunch when I noticed Squiggles and Rabbit staring straight at me outside the glass window. A moment later they disappeared. The girl was so beautiful, Squiggles quickly left my mind. We ate lunch and agreed to meet again in a couple of days. She even gave me her cell phone number without me asking. Wow, I was in heaven. This girl had the perfect face, the perfect body, she was rich, she was 28 and she was Japanese!

I walked back to the Park on cloud nine. I also realised I had spent my whole exposure time with Mariko. I felt guilty again. I spotted Rage and Jazz just about to finish my soda. I took off running and in one quick swoop I managed to grab the cup and gulp it down, all in one motion. I heard the guys laughing in the background. I tossed the cup, said my quick goodbyes and jogged all the way to the Telegraph bus stop. Just as I got there, I spotted my bus pulling out. Without breaking stride, I ran to the driver's door and beat on the window. The driver eventually stopped and cussed me out as I entered.

I knew if I was late again, questions might arise. I didn't want a counsellor going on my exposures with me, like they did with all the other patients. I liked going solo, for obvious reasons. It also hit me that I'd drunk after Rage and Jazz. I decided it was worth the risk of catching Aids. My life had been a living hell. If I got Aids, so be it. I would do anything to be able to live the rest of my life in peace.

This reminded me of another time I'd looked for peace: a

suicide attempt I'd made about 15 years ago. I'd stuck a potato in my exhaust pipe and waited for death to come. I ended up having a baked potato for dinner. One more failure to add to my low-self-esteem résumé.

A funny feeling suddenly came over me and snapped me out of my daydream. It was the feeling you get walking alone at night. I turned and looked out the back of the bus. My gut sank as I saw Squiggles waving goodbye to me. I finally realised that this wasn't some movie I was pretending to be in. It was a long ride back to the house.

COGNITIVE THERAPY

I ran into the house breathing heavily. It was lucky that I'd been a jogger for the last 20 years! Otherwise I would have been late for every class. Actually, I hated running but it offered some temporary relief from depression and anxiety.

'OK, James, you made it with five minutes to spare.'

It was Alley. She seemed to pop up everywhere I was. I started smiling.

'What's so funny, James?' said Alley.

'I don't know why but you just made me think about this girl in my travel-agent class years ago. I was a bit obsessive back then and every time the instructor would explain even the simplest things, I would end up asking her to repeat it, again and again and again.'

'Doesn't sound funny to me,' said Alley.

'I remember walking to my car on the last day of school and sitting on my bumper waiting for me was this little redhead who sat next to me in class. "Why did you always interrupt the class with all those stupid questions?" she said. I pondered a moment before replying, "I got an A+ on the final test. What did you get?"'

I waited a moment, setting Alley up for the conclusion.

'What did she say?' said Alley.

'She just jumped in her car and sped away!'

'Now that's funny!' said Alley.

We made our way to class as the usual warning of 'don't be late' was heard from the next room.

'Cognitive therapy: this is where the patient asks himself or herself, is the danger real? Is it logical that someone would walk up to you in a café and put something in your drink? Is it logical that touching a doorknob causes you to get infected with Aids? Or is it just magical thinking not based on reality?' said Martha, the therapist.

She was a pleasant-looking woman, about 50 years old. She was very meticulous, making sure everyone in the class understood it. She asked if anyone had heard of and applied that concept already. For some reason I decided to take a chance and open up. Maybe because Po' White and some of the others were not in this group.

'Martha, I touched this guy's hash pipe and a moment later I kept getting thoughts that this would make me high so I'd better go and wash my hands immediately. But another part of my brain kicked in and said, "That isn't rational. How can I get high just by touching it?"'

'Good, James! That is exactly how to use it,' said Martha.

I was feeling really good. I must have been confident if I'd mentioned my OCD in front of everybody.

'Yes, but policemen use gloves for just that reason,' said Barney.

I could tell by Martha's look that she despised Barney. Not personally, mind you, but he had been here in the past and upstaged her many times before, no doubt.

Martha quickly shot back with, 'If it was that easy to get

high, everyone in the street would pass the word and nobody would buy drugs.'

She was right. I had watched that *Cops* show on television many times and I remembered many of them picking up crack and all kinds of drugs without gloves on.

'Yes, Martha, that makes sense,' said Barney.

Martha looked exhausted as she spoke. 'Now, does anyone here not understand the meaning of cognitive therapy?'

I winked at Alley as I raised my hand.

MEL BROOKS

I got myself in trouble again bragging about Mel Brooks. I told everybody that Mel had invited Dr Swenson and me to LA to see his hit show *The Producers* for free. The problem was I had made it all up. It was one thing to bullshit Asian girls at Telegraph, but to tell tall tales at Within Reach was another story.

I guess it started when I called Mel from the house and told him where I was. I also let Teddy Bear get on the phone to talk to him. He was thrilled. I'm not sure if I did it for Teddy or if I did it for myself, to look like a big shot. Probably a little of both.

Next thing I knew I was going around telling everybody about the tickets. Then everybody was asking me if they could go with the Doc and me. Of course, I had to play the big shot and tell whoever asked me that they could go too. I knew I was in trouble when Po' White Trash asked me if he could go. I told him sure. My thinking was that nearly all the patients here were under a lot of medication. Thus they would be too anxious to go all the way to LA. Most were terrified of even going to the mall a few miles away. So, all in all, they would end up making some lame excuse as to why they couldn't go, and I would end up being top dog!

The truth was that if I were really invited with the Doc, Alley would be the only patient I would ask.

The Mel thing finally blew up in my face when Po' White Trash asked the Doc when we were going. The Doc told him he didn't know what he was talking about. Of course, Po' White came fuming into the dining room and yelled out in front of everybody that Dr Swenson had no idea about us going to see Mel's show. Luckily for me the Doc happened to walk by and I yelled out about how I'd mentioned about us maybe going to see *The Producers*. He kind of remembered something and said, 'Maybe we could all go and catch the train to LA.'

I was in trouble. Po' White had me. What was I going to do?

Out of nowhere, Amos yelled, 'If the train isn't too expensive!'

Good old Amos might have given me a way out. I knew he wasn't really worried about the money; he didn't want to miss a day at the Manor. Of course, I quickly jumped at that escape.

'I forgot about that. I'll check the prices on the Net.'

I had a feeling it would be at least a hundred dollars. Either way, that's what I'd be telling everybody. Luckily Po' White was computer illiterate, other than a few emails. Although I wasn't completely out of the woods, I decided not to mention Mel's name in the house again.

I guess the bottom line was I wanted people to think I was important. Or maybe I wanted them to like me. Mel was a lot like the Doc. They didn't present themselves as special people, but they were. I'm afraid they're an endangered species.

LEXUS

The trip to LA blew over. Did I learn a lesson? Probably not. The need to seem important superseded any risks. I began to think a lot about Alley. She was different from anybody I'd ever met. I had blocked one of her shots at basketball one night and yelled out to her and everybody in the gym that she should stick to the women's game. A few plays later she came all the way from the other side of the court to block one of mine. Everybody laughed at me but her.

We ended up agreeing to meet for coffee at Telegraph after my final group on Saturday afternoon. She had permission to skip all her groups on Saturday to attend to some business at San Francisco State University, so the plan was to meet in Berkeley at the academic bookstore. The security guard there was starting to follow me around the store so I was glad Alley was meeting me to keep me out of trouble.

I had a routine where I would visit three coffee shops in Telegraph Avenue for potential sightings of Asian women. I knew I was getting a reputation in the area but I couldn't stop myself. I somehow managed to keep justifying it with the fact I meant no harm and had made no outward sexual advances. Plus, if a girl showed no interest in having a conversation with me, I would quickly move away and try someone else. After all, I wasn't one of those guys who persisted even though a woman made it clear she had no interest.

I was going to catch the bus, but Eileen offered to give me a ride in her Lexus. I almost refused, because I looked forward to riding the bus in order to meet new women. I climbed in the car and wondered what I would say to Eileen to pass the time. I quickly found out that this wouldn't be a problem because she picked up her gay friend Adam. It didn't take long before they started in on everybody at the place.

'That guy with the yellow teeth stinks. I heard he didn't even have clothes when he came, that the staff had to go out and buy him some!' said Eileen.

Adam quickly chimed in: 'Yeah, I heard him say he was going to beat up another patient if he was threatened again. He wouldn't tell the counsellors who he was mad at, though.'

I quickly jumped in: 'Yeah, it must be me, 'cause I told him he stank so bad in basketball that I couldn't guard him!'

Everybody laughed.

Eileen said, 'I hear he has nine kids with six mothers and was disappointed that he had to give up his janitor job at the trailer park to come here.'

'I hear he killed someone during a quarrel over a liquor bottle in New York before coming here,' said Adam.

I burst out laughing. I knew these stories were untrue, but I wasn't about to spoil the party.

'He looks psychotic!' said Eileen.

Eileen then started on Amos and said, 'If that old bastard mentions that Homeward Manor one more time, I'm going to burn the goddamn place down!'

Adam said, 'I heard he's gay. He's 65 and never married. Matter of fact, he was winking at me at lunch the day I was released.'

'Yeah,' I said. 'He told me you were soooo cute!'

Everybody burst out laughing. I made that up about Amos. I knew for sure he wasn't gay. The others did too but it was funny talking about it. Then the conversation came to Alley.

Adam said, 'What is the deal with that black girl?'

Eileen said, 'Yeah, she thinks she knows everything.'

'You see the way she dresses!' said Adam.

I felt funny talking about Alley. I didn't mention I was on my way to meet her.

'Yeah, James, I see you talking to her. What is her problem?' said Eileen.

Of course, Adam jumped in begging to know her OCD too. It hit me that Alley was a good person and had helped me, whereas these two wouldn't flinch if a car hit me when I got out. I wouldn't have told them, even if I did know, which I didn't.

'It's none of my business what her problem is.'

There was a dead silence. A moment later the car pulled up by the academic bookstore. I thanked Eileen for the ride and climbed out. I knew as I turned around to walk to the bookstore that I would be the next patient talked about in the Lexus. I smiled. I felt a little extra bounce in my step as I opened the door to the store.

COFFEE WITH ALLEY

I felt a little weird as I walked into the academic bookstore and spotted Alley. I'd talked with her before, but mostly in short episodes. I was a little nervous about this one-on-one thing. I spotted her and made my way over to her table.

The first thing she asked me was how I'd got there. When I told her that Eileen and Adam had given me a ride, she said, 'Did they say anything about me?'

Now the right thing to do was say no. But that wasn't me. Plus, being in the house with all those people, I was sure my name came up more than most, so I was happy it had happened to somebody besides me.

'Adam said you were weird!'

Alley's jaw dropped. 'Why? What else did he say?'

'Well, they were talking about Amos and Po' White Trash and then your name popped up.'

'What did you say?'

'Yes, you are weird.'

'Thanks a lot.'

'Hey, I am weird too. Hell, everyone at Within Reach is weird,' I said. 'Those kinds of people talk about everybody. I'm sure they're talking about me now.'

Alley asked me if that was all they'd said and I told her yes. Just then, a Korean girl came up to me and said, 'Hey, I wait for you at Western Café yesterday and you never show up.'

To be honest I didn't even remember meeting the girl.

'Hey, my friend Alley here got sick and I had to take her to the hospital.'

'I thought maybe I can work on your documentary for the homeless, OK, James?'

I knew I had been making up some tall tales to the Asian women but I didn't remember this. I felt very uncomfortable.

'Well, I'll email you if I hear anything,' I said.

The girl walked away confused. I didn't blame her, because I had no idea what I'd meant by that last remark.

Alley took the opportunity to get back at me. 'So that's what you're telling all these women, James?'

'I have no idea where she got that; probably the language barrier. So, Alley, I never really thanked you for before. I didn't mean, you know, the thing about you being black.'

She told me she knew that already.

'What is your OCD, Alley?' I said.

'I have this obsession that I might be gay, among other obsessions. I'm not gay but my mind keeps saying, what if?'

I decided not to tell her about the similar feelings I'd had back in acting school in Hollywood: maybe because she might have thought I was always bragging about women to cover it up. If I was gay, I'd wasted a lot of years chasing women. I asked what her treatment was and she said they had her looking at naked women in *Playboy* to desensitise her. I noticed that she looked around a lot at other women when we were talking. I figured she'd probably end up in the Castro district of San Francisco a few years from now, living with some girl. I was also curious why, being from the West Coast, she was terrified of being that way. But I hoped I was wrong. Hell, I wish they had me looking at *Playboy*!

'You've never told me what your OCD is and why you're so obsessed with women,' said Alley.

'Listen, I don't want to talk about my OCD but as far as the women thing, I will tell you this: I've never felt love from anybody. Not as a boy and not as a man. I'm afraid I'm going to die without anybody ever loving me.'

I was starting to choke up but quickly got a hold of myself and changed the subject. I started bragging about all the women I had met since arriving here. Alley wasn't letting me off the hook that easily and persisted in trying to know something about me. I figured she had a little inclination about some of my fears because I'd admitted to being afraid of picking up that hash pipe at the Park. Also, she had admitted to eavesdropping on my sessions with Tonya. I touched on some small stuff then put the ball back in her court. She told me she also had a fear of germs and contamination. I think all of us had that to a degree. And her biggest fear seemed to be shared by most of the patients here: Aids.

I wondered why I had repeated what Adam had said about her. I knew she, like all the rest of us at Within Reach, was very insecure. I knew it would bother her, but I told her anyway. I always seemed to do cruel things to people who were nice to me. I was choking up again and needed a distraction.

'You know, Alley, my life is just a series of moments.'

'Meaning?' said Alley.

'Like when I walk over to a strange girl to meet her. There's always that possibility we might end up sharing a nice moment together. Even though deep down I know it won't amount to anything, I still like and need those moments.'

'What do you mean by moments?' said Alley.

'Anything. Like talking about life and sharing a few laughs. Like now. You and I are sharing a nice moment.'

'Why can't it amount to more than just a moment? Like friendships, for instance.'

I ignored Alley's question. I had changed the subject more than I'd planned.

After a long, awkward pause Alley said, 'Seeking a Series of Moments. Sounds like the title of a book.'

Speaking of moments, I noticed several cute Asian girls enter and leave the coffee shop. I literally got nervous every time an Asian girl got up and left. Each one might have been the answer to my search for the perfect woman!

Alley started asking me personal questions about my family. It was my fault for opening the door with my 'series of moments' theory. She was a sweet girl, but I was getting anxious and needed to approach one of the Asian women. I reminded myself that Alley had mentioned earlier she couldn't stay long because she had business to take care of.

I was just about to remind Alley about that when she got up and said she had to get going. I felt relieved and watched her walk to the steps. I couldn't wait any longer; I practically ran over to one of the girls and sat down. I started to recite my spiel when I saw Alley standing on the steps, shaking her head. She smiled and walked away. I realised I had sat with

Alley for an hour and hadn't shared much. I felt sad about that.

'Now, where was I?' I said with a fake smile to the Asian girl.

LINZY

Patients had come and gone since I'd arrived. Philly was gone too. I was getting better, but I wasn't ready to leave. Barney reminded me to change my anxiety-level scores every once in a while to fit in with the up-and-down pattern of most other patients. He told me they monitored that closer than we thought. Barney said that the staff would get together every Monday and go over the notes. The next three days I had a two for my day and an eight for my anxiety. Barney winked at me when I gave my scores. I even saw Amos shaking his head. They knew I was having a ball at Telegraph Avenue.

Of course, my bragging about all the women I had met didn't help things. The staff had to know I was still womanising. I knew Tonya said that three months was the going rate here, but I was shooting for four.

I was back on the computer when I heard the big guy yelling for everyone to report to the main room. I reluctantly got off the computer. The big fat guy was beginning to annoy me. I guess he'd found that actress's website or something and was obsessed with the computer.

I reluctantly walked into the room and was greeted by a new patient. She got up and told a little about herself. She was attractive and from Brazil. We went through the usual, telling our names and wishing her the best. Her name was Linzy.

Finally we broke for dinner. I noticed the Brazilian girl struggling with her suitcase so I went over to help her. I carried the suitcase up to her room, making sure the door was left wide open. 'If you enter the room of a member of the opposite sex, you leave the door open!' That was told to me on the first day.

I was about to leave when she said to me, 'I hope there's some sex in this place.'

Oh, man, I didn't need that.

A moment later she went on: 'I almost got laid at the airport by this lawyer dude. I didn't catch the cab here like I was supposed to. I had a couple of drinks with him and he ended up taking me to a hotel. After we got in bed, I changed my mind. You know, he was a sweet guy but I just changed my mind. Just before we closed the deal, I told him that I had a vision that he was a goat in his previous life and I tell you this, I'm not into bestiality! You wouldn't sleep with an animal, would you, James?'

I shook my head and told her I had to get going because it was my turn to do clean-up.

She called out to me as I exited her room, 'James, I asked that lawyer for his phone number and he told me he didn't have one. You'd think a guy with a Mercedes would have a phone, wouldn't you, James?'

I didn't reply, and headed down the steps. I had only talked to her for a couple of minutes, but I knew she was at the wrong place. She should have been up the hill at the psychiatric ward.

We had spaghetti for dinner. It was good. I was in a great mood after meeting Mariko. I told Amos and Barney I was in love. I was starting to connect with Amos. He was a real funny guy once you got him off the Homeward Manor kick. He said he had been a CPA (certified public accountant) at one time before the OCD. I was sure everybody in his hometown thought he was crazy just like me and the rest of us. I couldn't help but pick on him. I would say that Miss Davis, the big cheese at the Manor, was attracted to him because he was so macho. He had gone on earlier about how he'd had to move two full-size beds by himself. Truth was he would have had trouble lifting a toaster. If he was any more frail he would disappear.

I liked the fact that he was old and had no idea what drug-slang words were or anything related to that. 'Hey, Amos, I bet Miss Davis is in the shower fantasising about you right now. I'm sure she saw all that sweat dripping off that muscular body of yours when you moved that heavy furniture,' I yelled out across the dinner table.

Amos caught me off guard when he called back to me in front of the counsellors. 'Hey, James, how many girls' emails did you add to your collection? Last I heard you were at a hundred and counting. So, when are you going to see this new one: Mariko?'

Wow, I was in a spot. Everybody was staring at me. I quickly recovered. 'Yeah, I try and meet as many people as I can when we have down-time. I figure it's good exposure talking to strangers.'

Po' White said, 'Exposure for what?'

Everything got quiet so I just looked straight down at my plate, hoping it would pass. I looked up and noticed Alley and Amos winking at each other. I felt relieved for the moment, but that wouldn't last long.

'Boy, this spaghetti sauce tastes like marijuana,' a voice cried out.

I freaked out! Who had said it? I knew it came from the counsellors' area. So the jig was up: Dorwina was going for blood. I couldn't really blame her either after the insults, etc., etc. Yet maybe it was just by chance. I knew the only way to attack this was to fake bravery.

'Someone pass the spaghetti,' I quickly said. I tried not making any eye contact with the counsellors as I was passed the bowl. I filled my plate and gulped down a big fork full of spaghetti. I would show them! Out of the corner of my eye I spotted Dorwina. She was chatting with Mary and seemed to have no clue about the incident. I gulped down some more, spilling half of it on my shirt. I had stood and delivered. I grabbed the food off my shirt and ate it. Exposure – right!

I was about to get up and celebrate by emailing one of my babes when Linzy asked me if I'd spilt some food on my shirt and then eaten it. I told her I had. She then asked me why. I told her it was for no special reason and that I was just hungry. She nodded OK as I ran to the computer.

I was just getting in to my emails when I heard a voice whisper in my ear, 'You just ate that spaghetti even though it was on your shirt?' I turned around and it was Linzy. Oh, man. I knew exactly what was going on in her brain. She was asking for reassurance. I had done the same thing thousands of times. She then began repeating herself, again and again. The same thing with little different angles. In some selfish way, I was enjoying it. I felt the power thousands and thousands of people had had over me in the past. I knew it was wrong, but it felt so good coming from someone else. I reassured her over and over and I knew enough was never enough. Luckily the counsellors announced that the last group of the day was starting.

I enjoyed that group. It was split in half. One side went into the back room and mine stayed in the front room. My group had most of the good people in it: Barney, Amos and Teddy Bear. Philly had left the day before and it was nice that they'd had a party for him, cake and all. Linzy happened to be assigned to my group. Mary ran most of the meeting. When

Dorwina or one of her buddies took over, I didn't say a word. Barney dominated the talking and Mary, although somewhat annoyed, managed to laugh along with him. Of course, when they asked Amos how his day was, I knew the Homeward Manor would come up. His day was a ten and his anxiety was a zero, all because of the good old Manor.

In private I kept up my comments to Amos, like, 'I hear you're servicing Miss Davis.' I was afraid I was getting too close to Amos. I knew his days were numbered; perfect days and no anxiety was a sure ticket out. I knew I would have difficulty saying goodbye.

Linzy said her anxiety was a ten. Mary asked her why and she said she was obsessing about something another patient had said. I knew it was me, but I figured I shouldn't say anything. I was so happy Po' White was in the other group.

Anna was laughing and carrying on like she was at a party. When she said her anxiety was a ten, I lost it.

'Mary, how can anyone say they have a ten anxiety level and be laughing and carrying on?' I said.

Mary said that everybody was different and hid their anxiety differently. I didn't buy it. I'm also sure Teddy Bear didn't either. Now, when he said ten, he meant ten! He told Mary that his mind kept going back to whether he'd flushed the toilet or not. He was trembling. He told me he hadn't talked to the Doc yet about trying new medication. I don't know anyone who could go on the way he was. His hands shook constantly.

Something else suddenly caught my attention. I heard Linzy ask what time the curfew was. Mary told her ten and Linzy said she had time to catch the bus to Telegraph Avenue. I knew I should have minded my own business but something drove me to talk to Mary as I saw Linzy walk up the stairs.

'Mary,' I said, 'Linzy is not stable enough to be going down to Telegraph Avenue by herself.'

Mary asked me why.

I told her, 'Hey, I'm not a doctor but anybody can tell she's unstable.'

Truth was, I was just as unstable as Linzy or any other patient here.

She told me she would go and talk to her but she couldn't refuse her. If she wanted to go, she would go. Like I said before, this house was not part of the psychiatric ward.

I overheard Mary talking to her but it did no good. She tried telling her that the buses were pretty infrequent at night and that she would be in trouble if she didn't get back for curfew. Linzy rejected Mary's pleas and walked out the back door. I wondered why Tonya, who was her BT, hadn't spoken to her. I also wondered why I was getting involved.

SPAGHETTI

I fell asleep that night listening to the radio. I never could get to sleep without some kind of sound. My sister-in-law could just lie down anywhere and sleep for hours and hours. I was jealous of people like that. It meant to me that they had great childhoods. I, on the other hand, could remember Step-Mom Number One chasing my dad with a knife in the middle of the night.

I had finally fallen into a deep sleep when I heard a knocking sound at the door. I snapped out of my sleep and turned the radio off. The knocking continued. I figured it had to be two or three in the morning. I reluctantly opened the door and, before I could say anything, I heard, 'Why did you eat that spaghetti off your shirt, James?'

Oh my God, it was Linzy! She had just got home. She told me some guy from the bookstore had given her a ride. I reminded her if you're caught drinking even one beer, you're outta here! She just laughed and said she didn't drink.

A moment later the laughter stopped, as she went back to the spaghetti. I told her again that I ate the spaghetti off my shirt for no special reason. She told me she had been thinking about it all night at the bookstore. She also told me Igor was in the bathroom or something and hadn't noticed her slipping in. She continued the onslaught about the spaghetti. I reassured her again and again and again. Finally I told her to get to bed. She left reluctantly.

I turned over to go back to sleep. A moment later I heard a knock. To be honest I was expecting it. Linzy asked me again but managed to change the question just a little. I've thought many times that if my brain could be so exact about little details, I ought to be able to make millions using it for something positive.

Linzy snapped me out of my daydream. 'You said that you ate the spaghetti off your shirt for no particular reason, right?'

I nodded.

'What do you mean by "particular"?'

I reassured her I meant nothing special by that word. She said OK and left. I didn't move this time. I knew she would be right back. A moment later I heard a tap. I felt sorry for her. I also knew that Igor would be making his nightly rounds, and I didn't want to get into trouble for something I had nothing to do with. After all, I was on a short leash after having so many problems with staff and fellow patients. I would try a new strategy that had worked for me in the past.

'Listen: quit asking me these stupid questions and go to bed!'

It worked. She meekly shook her head and told me she was sorry for bothering me. I shut the door and felt good. It was strange, almost like looking in a mirror. I turned my radio back on and snuggled under the covers. I slowly started to drift back to sleep when I heard another tap on the door. I angrily got up and opened it. Linzy was standing there with pen and paper. She had written about ten questions and wanted me to answer yes or no to them. I did what she asked and sent her on her way. She again apologised and left the room.

It dawned on me how many times over the years I had done the same thing; how crazy everybody must have thought I was.

I took the headphones Philly had left and put them over my ears. I would not answer my door any more tonight. Linzy was on her own now. I also wondered if I would ever enjoy spaghetti quite as much as I used to.

TRIPPING

All the buzz the next morning was that another new patient had arrived. I had decided the best thing for me was to have a roommate. Yes, I'd had Philly, but he was so shy and meek it was almost like he wasn't there. I knew if I had any plans of getting married or even having a serious girlfriend, I would need to deal with someone being constantly around me.

I went down to the first group and was a little surprised to see most of the staff, including Dr Swenson, in attendance. Ralph was the new patient. He was Greek, and was in the import–export business. He was about 40, with jet-black hair that looked like it had been dyed with some shoe polish. He was as pale as a ghost and as skinny as a rail.

He introduced himself to the group. He spoke so fast that nobody could understand what he said, except his one last remark, 'Is this group about over? I need to make some phone calls concerning my business.'

Everybody burst out laughing. I mean, the guy hadn't been in the group two minutes and he wanted to leave to make a phone call. The counsellors scolded us. I kept thinking he would give Anna, Barney and even Amos a run for their money. He was wound up and wound up tight. His head was moving all the time. He would look at his watch, grab his stomach and then look around the room. He repeated things over and over.

Barney caught my attention. He was laughing at Ralph, too. I thought to myself, if Barney only knew how much he resembled this man's motions! We all did our usual spiel of what our goals were for the day. Amos was going to walk around plugging and unplugging desk lamps, to check they were OK – whatever the hell that meant. Teddy Bear was going to flush the toilet once, leave the room and not go back and check.

Now, I had my own cure for Teddy Bear. Amos was known to get up early in the morning and sit on the crapper relieving himself for at least an hour. Word was that it stank so bad when he left that it took hours to air out. Regrettably, house rules prevented us or the staff from using any type of air freshener. My solution would be to have Amos leave without flushing, then have Teddy Bear go in and flush it, the idea being that it would stink so bad that Teddy Bear couldn't bear the smell and would be unable to return. Thus he would be cured! Of course, to all the Triumph folks, that would be too simple. Oh well, it was just a thought.

It came to my turn and I said I would go to Telegraph and

the Park and not ask for any reassurance. Dorwina couldn't resist this opening I gave her.

'James, wouldn't that be setting yourself up for failure? I think you should allow yourself maybe two or three reassurances. That way you won't feel like a failure when you give in.'

The rest of the staff told Dorwina that she had given me great advice. I think I caught her winking at me.

'I've made a commitment to leave this place totally healed. Three times? Hell, even once is unacceptable to me,' I said.

Everybody clapped and yelled in jubilation for me. Even Dorwina, who was sitting next to Dr Swenson, was forced to clap. She couldn't have cared less if I'd got cured. I'm sure she was hoping I would get kicked out way before that happened. It also dawned on me that maybe Dorwina wasn't doing anything unusual and that I was just paranoid. Oh well.

I had been here a month now. I wanted to stay at least four, though deep down I knew I didn't deserve to. Sooner or later, I was bound to screw it up.

I remember the first day I had my OCD problem: I did LSD once in the '70s by accident. I was drunk and some guy told me he had got burned on some drug deal. He had bought some acid and it turned out to be sugar pills. He had taken five and nothing had happened. I asked him for one of the pills. I thought this would be my chance to go around acting cool, looking like I was dropping acid. The truth was I was terrified of drugs. I had been under a lot of peer pressure to try them but had managed to steer clear.

Fifteen minutes after taking the pill I was seeing giant pink rats. I took off, running down the street, trying to get away. That was the longest and scariest night of my life. It turned out worse for the other guy. I heard he was tripping for four straight days.

You would have thought I had learned my lesson. Not so. A week later I was with my friends, who were planning to trip together. I told them I wanted no part of that. They told me the only reason I had flipped out was that I wasn't with friends. I took the pill they gave me and put it in my mouth. I excused myself, ran into the bathroom, stuck my fingers down my throat and threw up. I drank a beer and prepared to do my first acting assignment. I figured it would be easy. Ten minutes later I was seeing fire in the sky!

That was the second-scariest night of my life. The only good thing to come out of it was that I decided I needed new friends. I also decided that no one would ever talk me into anything again!

I started getting depressed soon after. The somewhat positive thing was that I quit drinking. I say somewhat because I didn't quit because I wanted to, but because I was afraid that if I drank, I might start tripping again. My odd behaviour then began to manifest itself. I began having this irrational fear of the police. I thought if I spat on the sidewalk, I would get arrested. That lasted for many years.

When I went to Hollywood, it transformed itself into this fear of being gay. I was terrified whenever a gay person was near me. I could justify my fears somewhat since I'd never had a girlfriend for longer than a few weeks. It was made worse in acting school because there were all these macho guys who turned out to be gay.

It got so bad I went to a therapist. She encouraged me to try the gay lifestyle. Even in my darkest moments, when I was full of anxiety and depression, I knew that was wrong and would make things worse. She tried to get me onto tranquillisers but I was still afraid of pills because of my LSD experience and refused. It got worse when my therapist starting hugging me and eventually wanted to kiss me on the face. After all, I was in Hollywood, right, what else should I expect?

My anxiety got worse and worse. That, combined with the acting rejection, finally made me snap. Somehow I managed to get in my car and drive all the way back to Louisiana. The intense anxiety I was feeling made me hallucinate all the way back. It was a miracle that I didn't crash. It now seems surreal, like it happened to another person. I don't even think OCD was a diagnosis back then. I put it down to sheer chance that I've never been hospitalised.

Amos nudged me and snapped me out of my flashback. The group was over. He asked me if I was going on the ski trip to Sierra Summit, California, since that had come up last week during group. I thought about it, but it would mean being away from Telegraph all day for the first time since I'd been here. I'd become addicted to it. Plus, Po' White Trash and the big guy were going. It cost a hundred bucks all in, and I knew Po' White Trash's kids could use that money for clothes and food. I grew up poor and my dad always had these younger women he was spending money on but never spent anything on us kids. I knew I would think about that the whole trip and if I got near him, I would say something. I was on thin ice here anyway. Plus, Dorwina was going.

Amos wasn't going either. He was afraid they would fire him at the Homeward Manor. I tried to explain to him that volunteers don't get fired. Although he didn't admit it, I think he had a crush on Miss Davis. The highlight of his day was getting up in the morning and going there. Hell, that was the highlight of his life. I teased him a lot, but in truth I felt sorry for him. My OCD had perhaps been brought on by drugs or alcohol, but this man had never taken a sip of wine, let alone drugs. Now they had him on all sorts of drugs.

He told me he was going to be released next week. He had known about it for several weeks but was afraid to tell anyone. That hit me hard. Even though I'd avoided him at all costs at first – the Manor thing would drive me crazy – I'd got past that, and he was kind, sensitive and very funny. I wondered if he really would make it on the outside. I questioned him about that. He said he was terrified. Each day, as it got closer and closer, he got more anxious. I made a few jokes that he probably wouldn't make it past airport security because he looked so psychotic. He laughed, as usual. But I knew that deep down he was terrified. I knew I would feel the same way when my time arrived. No matter what happened, I too would get my date to leave.

PROGRESS

After being here a month I had made terrific progress. It was unbelievable. I had a meeting with Tonya before they took off for the ski trip. I had made arrangements to take Amos and Teddy to Fisherman's Wharf in San Francisco via the BART (Bay Area Rapid Transport). Although part of me wanted to go by myself so I could scam on some Asian girls, another part of me needed the friendship and interaction of these two oddballs.

Speaking of Asian girls, I was supposed to meet the rich and beautiful Mariko for lunch one day at the Western Café; even showed up a half-hour early to make sure I didn't miss her. For some reason I found myself drifting over to the academic bookstore and met a somewhat attractive girl and forgot all about Mariko. I called her the next day and told her I'd met another girl and forgotten about her. Of course, she cussed me out and said the Japanese don't do that to other people and that she had trusted me, even giving me her cell phone number.

I tried to figure out why I'd stood this beautiful creature up for a so-so-looking girl. It was like ordering a hamburger instead of prime rib when someone else was buying. My conclusion was that Mariko was way out of my league in many ways and that wouldn't have taken long to reveal itself. Oh well.

I opened the door of Tonya's office and walked in. We had decided at an earlier meeting to try to reconstruct my LSD experience by my visualising it and talking her through it, but I wasn't sure exactly why. I tried to tell her I wasn't in the mood and it would be better if we waited until next time. The fact was I was stalling for time. I didn't want them to realise how much progress I had made and kick me out early. They were always telling me how many people were waiting to get in.

'Are you sure about the three-month limit, Tonya? Amos has been here six months so I was thinking I should at least get four months.'

My theory was if I asked for four, I would at the very least get three, maybe three and a half.

'Amos is an unusual situation. He couldn't walk or talk when he first got here.'

I asked Tonya if I would definitely stay for at least three months. She said that it all depended.

'You mean, if you're not quite well at three months, maybe you will get a fourth to complete your treatment?'

'You're obsessing, James, so let's move on to another subject. Are you ready to flashback to your LSD trip?'

I started to ask for reassurance about what she'd just said. I was tempted, but I didn't have that overwhelming feeling I once had.

'Well, I would rather do it next week. Oh, by the way, are your kids going on the ski trip?'

She reminded me that I always changed the subject. I started recalling the events of one or both of my acid trips, since I was somewhat confused as to which one was which. 'I'm seeing colours; I'm running in the rain; I think this will never end.'

I didn't really feel anything while telling her this. I feigned a little just to make her happy. Eventually she gave up on the experiment. She told me to get Hunter S. Thompson's book *Fear and Loathing in Las Vegas* and read it, hoping it would cause me some anxiety which would lead to desensitisation. I also told her that I'd had Grand Funk Railroad's music playing in my house on the nights I was tripping. They were a successful rock group in the early '70s. I told her that, from then on, whenever their music came on, I would immediately change stations. She told me to go and buy their tape and play it. At the end of the session she told me that after she got back from the ski trip, she would put something in my cereal and make me eat it.

'What? I ain't eating no cereal if you put something in it!'

'Listen, James, we will never do anything to harm you. We would be closed down if we did unethical things like that.'

'Oh, I see. You're going to pretend there is something in my food, right?'

She didn't respond and said my time was up. I walked out a little shook up. I knew she couldn't put anything in it but I still felt a little nervous.

My next meeting was with Jimmy. I had played real physical in the last night's basketball game with him and he hadn't said anything. We kind of took turns shoving each other but no words of any kind were spoken. I didn't like him any more. I was anxious as I opened the door and sat down.

'Wow, you look like shit, man, did you get any sleep last night? You didn't take anything, did you?' said Jimmy.

I wanted to punch his lights out. Of course, he knew I would be asking for reassurance within seconds. I decided right then and there that I wasn't going to give in to the bastard. Instead, I challenged him. 'I think you know the reason I pushed you around and didn't talk to you last night at basketball, don't you?'

He was caught off guard. He was waiting for me to turn into putty and start begging for reassurance. A month ago I would have.

'I knew you were pissed last night when you wouldn't speak to me. So, no, I'm not sure why. Let it out,' said Jimmy.

I was confused. I wanted to tell him off big time. He had let me down at the Doc's office. I also knew if I went overboard, I'd be history. Although the Doc had said I would never get kicked out, I realised I had a lot of anger towards Jimmy and needed to let it out.

'Jimmy,' I said. 'I thought we were friends.'

He made me face something I'd been avoiding: 'You're the one telling the counsellors off, not me.'

It hit home. He was right. I just didn't want to admit it was my fault. We exchanged some small talk and, before I knew it, my time was up.

I walked out and headed towards the house. Unfortunately it didn't take long before I started thinking about something he had said. 'You didn't take anything last night, did you?' It played over and over in my head. Son of a bitch! My mind started up like it had in the past. Over and over again! I knew if I went back in there I might as well sit on the floor and let him piss on my face. He could do anything he wanted. But I was powerless to resist. I turned around and walked back into his office to get my fix: reassurance.

As I opened the door, he blurted out, 'Hey, James, I don't want to say anything that will make you go overboard. I mean, I'm trying to help you get well but I don't want to make you go over the edge.'

He had given me reassurance without me asking. My anxiety level dropped about nine points.

'Did you forget something?' he said.

I asked him if I had left my glasses. Of course, he said no. I had a half-assed smile as I walked back to the house. It sank in finally that he was on my side.

SKI TRIP

Everybody left for the ski trip except Amos, Teddy and me. Of course, they had a part-time counsellor holding down the fort.

Eileen didn't want to ride in the crowded bus with all the peons and used some lame excuse that it made her claustrophobic. She got permission to drive her Lexus to the ski lodge with some of her friends from Stanford. Amos and she had recently had a falling out when he'd refused to carry several boxes up the stairs after she had gotten home from another clothes-shopping spree. Amos claimed to have a bad back but the guy probably couldn't or wouldn't admit he was too weak and frail to carry them. Word was she'd called him a little faggot. Teddy Bear had agreed to come to Fisherman's Wharf if Amos came too, so I decided to use this information to get him on board. I did wonder why I was bothering, because I would have had the whole day to myself to chase women. But companionship won out and I was determined to get Amos to go with me – for laughs, if nothing else.

I walked up to him as he was sitting on the couch and said, 'Eileen told me you never leave this place because you're a closet homosexual and you're afraid if you see a man walking on the street you won't be able to control your impulses and will try and pick him up!'

Amos muttered something like 'that witch', but I didn't get the response I wanted. I went in another direction.

'I told Eileen I was taking you and Teddy to Fisherman's Wharf for lunch and sightseeing and she laughed right in my face and said that little bastard would never go. She said she wanted to burn down the Homeward Manor and that phoney Miss Davis with it, too!'

'Miss Davis is the kindest woman I have ever met! I mean, she treats me like I'm one of the team. Miss Davis is top notch. I mean, she treats every person there like royalty.'

'Not according to Eileen.'

'I'll show Eileen!'

Amos immediately jumped out of his chair and was ready to go on our big day out to San Fran. I couldn't remember if Eileen had said any of those things or not but I figured they were the kind of things she would say. Me, him and Teddy Bear took off down the street to catch the bus to the BART. It didn't take long before Amos started up.

'Are you sure we can catch the bus back? Because I've never been late or been written up in six months!'

I told him that we would get back in plenty of time. We went into the doughnut shop to wait for the bus. Amos soon moved on to the subject of the good old Homeward Manor.

'You know, James; the Homeward Manor is not only the top nursing home in Berkeley but in the whole United States. Did I tell you how kind Miss Davis is to all her patients? I mean, it don't matter how rich you are, she treats them all the same. Did I tell you the guy who founded Wal-Mart is in there?'

The guy who founded Wal-Mart had passed away, so I knew he wasn't in there, but I didn't want to ruin his fantasy.

'Hey, why didn't I go to work today? I have to turn around. Miss Davis will need me,' said Amos.

The truth was that Amos was finished there and would be leaving Within Reach in three days' time. I had a funny feeling in my gut. Although I had been fluctuating as to whether Amos would make it or not on the outside, this last remark made me think for certain he would end up bedridden like he was before coming here. I had laughed like everybody else whenever he went off on the Homeward Manor spiel. I think I was starting to feel guilty about that.

'Hey, Amos, why don't you just move here and get a steady job volunteering at the Manor?' I said.

'Detroit is my home; I need to go home.'

'Home to what, lying in bed by yourself all day?'

Amos didn't reply. He must have felt some security back in Detroit. Or maybe he was afraid of making a decision. Teddy Bear broke the silence.

'Hey, you like the Rangers, Amos?'

I knew it was going to be a weird day on the streets of San Francisco. A moment later the bus pulled up and we were on our way. We got off at the subway and caught the BART to Montgomery St Station, for the Market St bus to Fisherman's Wharf. Amos and Teddy were both uncomfortable riding the BART, but I, on the other hand, loved the whole experience. I loved the Bay Area too. I had been to many places in my life, but this was it. I knew if I really got better, I would like to live somewhere around the Bay.

I spotted a young Caucasian woman sitting near Teddy. My plan was to get my travelling buddies to approach an unaccompanied woman somewhere in San Fran today. I figured it would be good for their psyche to be able to do that and would give them some self-confidence. On the other hand I was probably showing off what an expert I supposedly was with women. I also figured that, at the very least, it would be funny. I nudged them both to watch me in action. I moved over to the woman next to Teddy and started my spiel.

'Hi, I'm from New Orleans and I'm usually a little shy, but you're so attractive I couldn't help but say hello.'

I winked at the guys and continued. 'I find myself only attracted to Caucasian women because y'all are so beautiful and sexy. I was thinking you could join me for lunch and maybe show me around the city. What do you say, honey?'

I was grinning from ear to ear. I knew the guys were wishing they had the confidence I had. The girl finally mumbled something but I couldn't understand her. I looked over to the guys, who were mesmerised. I spoke to the girl again. 'Hey, honey, what did you say?'

Now I don't usually use the word honey, but I was going over the top, showing off to the guys. The girl finally spoke clearly.

'Sir, you're old enough to be my father.'

The subway stopped and the woman quickly got off. I was devastated. I wasn't that old, was I? I looked over at Amos and Teddy, who were laughing their asses off. I felt real bad. Like somebody had punched me in the stomach. Finally our last stop came and we got off. Teddy looked at me and broke the ice.

'Sir, why did you say you only like white women when you're white too? It sounded kind of silly.'

We all laughed together. I realised they weren't laughing at me but with me. Of course, even I had to admit how lame my lines were. I must have used one of my Asian lines by mistake. 'Now you see why I only like Asian and Spanish women. They aren't rude like she was,' I said.

Amos and Teddy nodded. Of course, they had no idea what I was talking about. These two couldn't pick up a hooker in Vegas. A monk in Nepal had more experience with women than them. We made our way to Fisherman's Wharf and found a strip kind of mall full of food places. We chose Japanese and sat down to eat. As we were finishing up, I noticed a gal of about 60 sitting by herself. I waited till the old woman was just about through before sending Amos over to talk to her. He, of course, was scared and refused to go.

'Well, Amos, I guess I'm going to have to tell Eileen it's true about you being gay and terrified of women.'

'I'm not gay; it's just that I don't find that woman very attractive.'

'I promised to tell Eileen what happened today since she promised to give me a ride to Telegraph Avenue on Saturday in return. I guess I'll have to tell her you were scared to talk to a woman.'

Amos immediately jumped up.

'OK, but what do I say to her?'

'Tell her she looks like your ex-wife. Now, let the ex settle in before you hit her with, "Unfortunately, she just passed away from cancer."'

'Why let the ex settle in, James?'

'First, she finds out you're single and available, then the widow line jolts her. Before she knows it, she's feeling sorry for you. Now get over there before she leaves. Oh yeah, don't mention the fricking Homeward Manor!'

I couldn't believe it. He slowly walked over to her table and sat down. I was in heaven. I knew none of the counsellors at the house could have accomplished this feat in a million years. Yes, I had talent! I watched them as they were having an actual conversation. I was a genius.

Now to get Teddy one. I looked around till I spotted a little Asian gal. I knew from my experience that Asian women were generally very polite and would talk to anybody out of courtesy, if for no other reason. I started my spiel on Teddy, saying Po' White Trash and the big guy were laughing at him just the other day and were making remarks like, 'Teddy has the personality of a cucumber and is so boring he could put people to sleep at an ADD convention.'

Teddy got angry and said he would talk to the girl as soon as he'd used the bathroom. As he left, I kept my eye on Amos. He smiled at me with a new-found confidence. Wow! I had to know what he was talking about. I slowly snuck around to the other side until I got close enough to eavesdrop. I leaned over and heard Amos speaking.

'You know the Homeward Manor is the best nursing home not only in Berkeley but in the whole world.'

Oh, Jesus, the fricking Homeward Manor!

I looked at the woman. She almost seemed enamoured by what Amos was saying. Oh, Lord, I was thinking. She gave desperate, bored and lonely a whole new meaning. That said, I took a step back and kind of patted myself on the back. I decided to buy a Dr Pepper to celebrate. I stood around and surveyed the mall. I noticed the woman that I had picked for Teddy getting up to leave. Now, Teddy had been gone for a while so I figured I'd better go and check on him. I went downstairs to the restroom and noticed a long line waiting to get in. I looked around for Teddy, but he was nowhere in sight. Worried, I walked up to the front of the line and was about to ask someone what was going on when I suddenly heard the sound of a toilet flushing.

And after a couple of minutes, I heard it again. At this point some guy had had enough, and he started yelling for security.

Oh no! I banged on the door and yelled, 'Come out, Teddy, I know you're in there!'

I heard someone in the background yell again to get security. I tried again. 'Teddy, please open the door, the cops are coming.'

A moment later Teddy slowly opened the door. I quickly climbed in and closed the door behind me. 'What the hell is going on, Teddy?'

'I keep checking the toilet to make sure I've flushed it.'

People began pounding on the door again.

'We've got to get out of here, Teddy.'

'I can't until I'm positive I've flushed it.'

I knew I had to do something quickly. The pounding was getting louder. I grabbed Teddy's arm, pulled him over to the toilet and flushed it.

'You saw me flush it, Teddy. Now let's get out of here!'

I grabbed his arm and headed for the door. He suddenly stopped.

'I need to go back just one more time and make sure it's flushed, James.'

I knew once would never be enough. I grabbed his arm and pulled him out the door. As we got to the steps, Teddy stopped me.

'James, how can I ever have a normal life if I can't stop thinking about the toilet?'

'Listen, Teddy Bear, get hitched up with some cute Asian girl and she'll flush the toilet over and over for you.'

Teddy smiled. We finally made our way back to the food court. Amos was sitting alone at our table. I quickly went up and patted him on the back.

'Nice job, Amos! Where's your honey? I am sooooo proud of you!'

Amos looked up. 'She was a deaf mute and didn't understand a word I said.'

I fell on the floor in laughter. Maybe for once in her life the woman should be glad that she was deaf and didn't have to hear about the Homeward Manor.

'Hey, it's a start,' I said to Amos as I patted him on the back, trying to control my laughter.

We decided it was late and we'd better head home. I told the guys I needed to use the restroom before we headed out. The tacos we had at the house last night must have kicked in and, after being constipated half the time from the meds I was on, I was always thrilled when I had the urge to use it. I told the guys to sit at the table and not move. I was going to try to find a bathroom quickly because an emergency was near. I knew the one Teddy had backed up was no good so I walked up another flight of stairs.

Just as I hit the top floor I got distracted by a shoe store. I admit I probably have a shoe fetish, because the first thing I look at when I notice a woman is her shoes. In my experience a woman with cool shoes is usually a cool person. More importantly than that, she probably has cute feet.

I quickly looked in as I passed. Oh my gosh! Did I see what I thought I saw? I quickly backed up and looked again. A beautiful Asian girl was trying on these great boots. She was about 25, I guessed, and Japanese. I forgot about my bodily functions for the moment and walked in. I worked my way over to her and started my spiel.

'Those boots look great on you. I bought my ex-girlfriend from Tokyo a pair just like them.'

Again I wasn't sure she was Japanese but I was getting good at picking them out.

'You have been to Tokyo?' she said.

'Oh yeah, I lived with my ex-girlfriend for about a year there. We lived near the airport.'

'Where? I live near the airport too.'

Oh boy. What do I say to that? 'Uh, close to uh, the United Airlines terminal.'

'Wait, there isn't any place to live there besides a hotel, is there?'

'Are you psychic, because I lived out of a hotel there.'

'Wow, you sound like an interesting man.'

'You have no idea, my friend,' I said, with a shit-eating grin on my face.

I must have done something right because the next thing she was telling me was she had come over here to California to go to school at Berkeley. We ended up chatting and exchanging names as she bought the boots. I asked her for her email address and told her I was from Los Angeles, here doing research on the homeless.

'Why not do the research in LA, as there are many homeless people there, aren't there?'

She had me on that one. 'We think it's better to do it here in northern California because it's colder and rains a lot more. The homeless have to deal with the elements.'

'Makes good sense to me,' said the sweet Japanese girl.

I even had to pat myself on the back for giving such a great answer.

'Wow, that is very interesting work, James. Listen, I have to catch the Muni Metro to North Beach. Would you like to join me?'

I knew I needed to get back to the guys. I also knew if I let this beautiful creature go, I would probably never see her again.

'It's up to you, James, but the Metro leaves in two minutes so we have to hurry!'

I smiled and took her hand as we headed off together. It suddenly hit me that those two guys couldn't find their way around Within Reach, let alone the city of San Francisco. But I was powerless under the spell of a beautiful woman. Of course it would be good for those two to find their own way home, I reasoned.

THE LONG WAY HOME

I spent the evening with the beautiful Japanese girl. We made our way around the bars of North Beach and ended up having dinner at this fancy restaurant in Union Square. If you're not from California, it's similar to Rodeo Drive in Beverly Hills. The kind of place where the rich and beautiful hang out and buy things to impress each other. I was neither rich nor beautiful, but I was playing the part this night.

I fed her my usual line of crap. I even got caught out on a couple of lies but this gal was straight from Tokyo so I could cover them somewhat with, 'Oh, you misunderstood me.' One lie begets another lie, and before you know it you're covered with them. I justified it to myself by thinking, 'This girl is way out of my league, so I have to lie.'

It dawned on me a few times that I shouldn't have left the guys, but one look at this lovely gal's face made me forget. She also said something to me I'd never heard before: 'You have yellow fever if you only like Asian girls!' Wow! I guess I was afflicted with that. She laughed when she said it so it must be good, I thought.

Before I knew it, it was nine-thirty. I couldn't make it home on time taking the BART to the bus connection. I got the girl's email and caught a taxi all the way back. I had already made my mind up that I'd never break the curfew. I think maybe a little of it was my OCD and another part of it was that I didn't want them to have any weapons to hold against me in case I did anything else wrong.

As we were driving home, I looked out of the window for the guys, but I knew I couldn't be kicked out of Within Reach for whatever happened to them. After all, they were adults and, technically, I wasn't responsible for them. Of course, morally was another matter.

We drove up to a stop sign and a pizza driver pulled up next to us. It took me back to the beginning of last year, when I'd ended up working in a pizzeria. My depression had been so bad before this that I was constantly fantasising about getting a gun and ending it all. The compulsion would let up momentarily, but would return a few minutes later. Luckily for me I had a walking partner back then who seemed to naturally calm me down without even knowing fully about my problems. But the calming effect would always wear off. He'd get onto a subject like sport, or something, and my mind would go right back to getting a gun.

I talked about suicide in general to see what he had to say. He surprised me by confessing that when he was younger and things were going bad financially, he had one day reached for a gun. He'd thought his family would have been better off with the insurance money. His dog had jumped on him when he'd reached for his rifle. That had somehow jolted him out of it. Of course, now he was successful and happy. I wanted to tell him about my thoughts. I hesitated, though. Even though he was a nice man, I somehow felt he might not understand and it might backfire. For the same reason I never told Mel Brooks about wanting a gun either. I was frightened that I would put them both off talking to me and lose the only two people in the world that I had any regular communication with.

Day after day my depression and anxiety got worse. I even emailed this Christian girl, Jen, who I'd met doing the PBS movie, and said my goodbyes to her, thanking her for all the kind words and emails she had sent me over the last two years.

I drove down a street that I remembered having a gun store on it somewhere. As fate would have it, the store turned out to be right next to a pizza place that was advertising for driver help. I thought for a moment. I figured I could always buy the gun tomorrow. I walked in and they hired me on the spot. I took the job, but had problems catching on to the little things: like how to find the houses to deliver the pizzas! My depression and anxiety were so strong that I couldn't understand any of the directions the manager had written for me. That, combined with the heavy prescription drugs I was taking, made me walk around like a zombie. I'm sure all the employees thought I was just plain stupid. I preferred that to the truth: that I was severely depressed and suicidal. I mean, I used to get anxiety attacks on my deliveries. They didn't fire me, though. That showed me two things: one, that any moron can deliver pizza; and two, they have trouble finding morons to deliver pizza! It turned out to be only a matter of time before I'd end up getting a gun, of course.

I was quickly knocked back to reality when I recognised two men standing at a random street corner back in Berkeley. It was Amos and Teddy. I told the cabbie to pull over and pick them up. They told me they'd lost their money for the subway and the bus ride back home.

'Where were you, James?' said Amos.

'I'm sorry, guys, but I had an anxiety attack back at the mall, and before I knew it, I had walked a couple of miles and I didn't know where I was!'

'We were worried about you. We stayed there looking for you for hours and hours,' responded Teddy.

'I'm sorry, guys, but I couldn't help myself.'

That part was true. I literally did have an uncontrollable disease. I asked them how they'd got this far and they said they'd hitchhiked.

'This will be the first time I've ever missed the curfew!' said Amos.

Well, I owed him that much. I told the cabbie to hit the gas, and that I'd throw in an extra ten if he got us home within five minutes. As expected, as soon as we got moving, Amos started obsessing about the time. It was seven minutes till ten and we were about six city miles away.

The guys needed cheering up. 'Hey, you two should be really proud of yourselves today! I mean, Amos, you talked to a woman, and you both hitchhiked from San Fran at night, no less. I must say, even I wouldn't have the balls to do that!'

They both looked at each other in agreement. I was feeling good as we got closer and closer to the house.

'Hey, driver, you must go to the Homeward Manor a lot, huh?' said Amos.

I signalled to the driver to say no but it was too late.

'Yeah, I do,' said the driver.

'Did you know that it's not only the best nursing home in Berkeley but . . .?'

STANDING TALL

We made it home for curfew that night and Amos was thrilled about that. The following day I was back at People's Park doing my thing, talking to Rage and Jazz, who were begging for a bottle of vodka. I left them when I spotted this guy in a wheelchair holding on to an oxygen bottle. I had seen him around and felt sorry for him. I had laid a little money in his cup earlier but hadn't had a conversation with him. My mission that day was to get his story. Everybody living on the streets has a story. I wanted his.

I walked up and made small talk. A moment later he was offering me a sandwich. I didn't want it for multiple reasons. The man was dirty and probably a drug addict. I was confronting both my germ and my drug fears. He kept insisting I eat it because someone had given him two and he wasn't hungry and was going to throw it away. I told him no, that I wasn't hungry, but I kept thinking about what the Doc had said about taking chances if one wanted a happy and productive life. I grabbed the sandwich and ate it as fast as I could.

The next thing I knew I was knocked down from behind! 'Why the fuck are you eating his food?' said Squiggles.

I looked up and Squiggles was standing straight over me. I wanted to grab the bastard but held my temper back. I slowly got to my feet and told him the old man had insisted I eat it because he didn't want it. The old man concurred. That didn't help. Squiggles knocked me back down again. What could I do? Tell him I was a patient at Triumph? He finally walked away from me and whispered something in the old man's ear. Oh, God, my mind took off. What if Squiggles had put some crack in the sandwich for him and now I'd eaten it? I needed reassurance from the old man and I needed it fast!

I stood around waiting for Squiggles to leave but he didn't. Finally Squiggles spotted the young boys from before and took off after them to make some drug deal. I started over towards the man in the wheelchair. Suddenly the sun, my only constant ally, popped out. The urge for reassurance disappeared. I'd never had this kind of confidence in my whole OCD life! I walked away and headed for the bus stop on Telegraph. The sun shone brighter than it ever had.

I made a promise to myself at that very moment: someone would be pushing drugs to kids in People's Park when I left Berkeley, but it wouldn't be Squiggles!

THE PHONE CALL

I was in a great mood as I entered Within Reach. Keeping it together with the old man and Squiggles was something I couldn't have comprehended just weeks ago. I did the rounds and found out that one of the girls was leaving the next day and there was a party. I guess Eileen had bought one of those expensive cakes from the bakery with her dad's credit card. I wondered who would buy me a cake.

The girl who was leaving had never got better. I heard on the grapevine that her depression was so severe she was doing shock treatments. I went in and joined the party. Po' White Trash was acting like a big shot. One of the girls had dyed his hair. Now I had one more reason to dislike him: I hated red hair. He and the fat guy were flapping around Mary like moths round a flame.

This reminded me of something. Many times my depression was so overwhelming that I began praying to God to give me a heart attack. But then a moment later a beautiful woman might walk by, and, even in the deep, dark place I was in, I would jump up and start flirting with her. I would think how crazy it was, but at least I had something to give me temporary relief. Most people had nothing.

Someone snapped me out of my thoughts by telling me I

had a phone call. I was thinking it was Ray Ray, and walked quickly to the phone. It was my brother. He told me that my mother was in intensive care and had almost passed away a few minutes ago, but they had revived her. I said 'oh' and then changed the subject to me and how I loved Berkeley and how I was getting better. I hung up the phone after saying something like, 'She *would* get better.'

I walked back to the party and told Amos about the call. His immediate response was, 'You have to go back home. It's your mother.'

I told him I wasn't that close to her. He insisted I go, telling me that I would feel terrible if she died and I wasn't there. I dismissed him. Deep down I knew he was right. To be honest I was getting better and I didn't want to give up all the women I had met. I knew this was sad, but that's the way I felt. I left the dull party and went upstairs to listen to my radio. I didn't sleep well. I tossed and turned. I was glad I had an appointment with Tonya the next day.

We went through the usual rounds after breakfast. I couldn't sit still during the first therapy group and slipped out the side door. I walked outside and started crying uncontrollably. I walked over to Tonya's office and hoped she was there, even though our meeting was a half-hour away. Luckily she was alone. She let me in because I was still weeping. She asked me what was wrong.

'Listen, my mother is dying. I harassed my mother her whole life. I called her a bitch and told her she was no good and I was fucked up because she gave me up when I was five and that I couldn't have relationships with women because of her and I blamed my OCD on her. I hated her guts; I couldn't stand the sight of her. I'm sorry; I haven't cried in the last 20 years, but this guilt thing is eating me up. I was really bad when I was drinking. I told her terrible things!'

'You were drunk when you did it, so . . .'

'No! I did it when I was sober too! I hated her guts. She would give me money all the time to try to make up for it but I hated her even more for that. If she dies without me telling her I'm sorry, I don't know if I can handle that.'

The phone rang, interrupting our conversation. I heard Tonya say 'good' and that she would tell me. She hung up and told me she had good news: my brother had called and said that my mother was out of CCU and in a stable condition. It was as if somebody had flipped a switch. I immediately stopped crying. I told Tonya I didn't want to talk about that subject any more.

'It's OK to cry, James. It's good to let it all out. Also, keep this in mind: there are consequences for everything we do in life.'

'Meaning?' I said.

'I know you feel bad about the way you treated your mother but when she gave you up as a child there were consequences.'

A light went on in my head. She said the magic word: consequences. I felt a lot of guilt leaving my body. Of course, I wish I hadn't treated my mother that way, but, as Tonya said, there are consequences for everything.

Tonya snapped me back to reality by saying, 'So, tomorrow at breakfast I'm still going to put something in your cereal before you eat it, as we had planned.'

I nodded OK. She then asked me how I was doing at Telegraph and the Park. I told her it was fine and that I was meeting scary people every day and getting better.

'Are you still sticking to the plan and not drifting away from it with women?'

'Of course. That's why I'm here, right?'

She looked at me slyly and told me avoidance was another

form of OCD. I had planned to avoid Kenny after our bizarre meeting but she was right, I needed to look for him every time I went to Telegraph. I would give him some change next time and see what trip he took me on, so to speak.

I told Tonya about Squiggles and the gang almost as if I were pitching a movie. I had lived in a fantasy world for so long that sometimes it was hard to distinguish fiction from reality.

I had to if I wanted to survive.

HANGING WITH RALPH

Ralph was quite a guy. He felt some connection with me, probably because we were close in age. He even brought me to his room to show me some old pictures of himself when he was working out. I didn't have the heart to tell him he looked exactly the same as he did now.

'Hey, Ralph, you look like Tyrone Power, the old movie star!' I said.

'Tyrone Power the great Greek movie star! Oh, thank you, thank you, you are so kind!' said Ralph.

'I don't think he's . . .'

Before I could finish he was back on the telephone.

'Sir, I'm Ralph Habba, and I'm a very important businessman, and − no, don't hang up on me. I look like Tyrone Power, the Greek movie star! No, don't connect to that anti-Greek music because I . . . no, the last guy hung up on me too! Hello? Hello? . . . Damn, the bastards hung up on me again!'

He then proceeded to get back on the phone and do the exact same thing.

'Sir, I'm Ralph Habba and I want to know my account

balance and my number is 27722222! Yes, no, I don't want to be left on hold, sir. I'm a very good customer, and – damn, they hung up on me again! They know I'm Greek! I am calling the Greek embassy and reporting them.'

Tyrone Power didn't sound Greek to me but then again neither did Ralph Habba. And he didn't look like Tyrone, either. He finally hung up the phone and approached me. 'Hey, Bob, let's go get something to eat. This prison food is killing me!'

I didn't have the heart to tell him my name was not Bob. I knew he wouldn't last a week here. Before I could say anything, Linzy came by and said she'd heard Ralph inviting me to dinner and she wanted to go too. I felt I had something to do at the house, but it wouldn't come to me.

Ralph must have had money because we drove to a Greek restaurant in a Mercedes convertible. I thought this might be a fun night as I watched Ralph talk to the owner in Greek but to my despair he quickly made his way over to the pay telephone.

'Doesn't Ralph remind you a little of Amos?' said Linzy.

Now I remembered what had bothered me before I left the house. This was Amos's last night! I had wanted to spend some time with him because he was the only guy I really related to. I knew I should have remembered. I went over to Ralph and interrupted his phone call, saying, 'This is Amos's last night; we need to get back right now before the party ends!'

'Party? I want to party!' said Linzy.

Ralph actually listened to me and hung up the phone. A few moments later we were speeding down the road. Ralph drove like he spoke: fast!

'I bet Ralph knows how to party,' screamed Linzy, to oncoming traffic. A moment later she ripped off her blouse and threw it in Ralph's face, blinding him. I quickly slid under the seat, holding on for dear life. A couple of months ago I would have welcomed death, but now I desperately wanted to live!

Somehow Ralph slammed on his brakes and ended up on a dead-end road.

'Linzy, you need to have more respect for yourself. Is this the way you want to present yourself to new friends? People will respect you only if you respect yourself,' said Ralph.

Wow! I was impressed. Ralph had class, character and decency. I, on the other hand, tried not to look at her boobs. Unsuccessfully. A few moments later we were back at the house, safe and sound. Ralph gave Linzy a sweater from his car. I had a whole new respect for Ralph.

I wandered into the kitchen expecting the party to be still going on. I was surprised when I didn't see anybody. The table was clear, too. I went upstairs to Amos's room to see what was going on. I was surprised to see him slumped over his bed.

'My last night here and nobody even threw me a party. Tonya was downstairs right before I came up and didn't even say goodbye or wish me luck.'

I felt bad for Amos. I knew Tonya would have said goodbye if she was aware he was leaving. I, on the other hand, had known all week that he was going and hadn't bothered to do anything. No, I wouldn't have bought him one of those expensive cakes like that rich girl always did. But I might have got him one at the supermarket.

I thought of a way of cheering him up. I asked him about Miss Davis and the Manor. I told him I was going over there tomorrow to try to volunteer – something I would never do, but I knew it would get Amos's attention.

'You wouldn't like that job, James. It's very depressing.

155

All those old people in wheelchairs sitting there half out of their minds. No, James, you wouldn't like it. You're too happy and upbeat for that. That job would bring you down.'

Wow. Amos really had to be down to be talking negatively about the Manor. I would have to try another approach.

'Hey, Amos, if you moved here like I told you before, you could get a job at the Manor and see Miss Davis every day. I heard she was lonely. Her husband died very recently, you know.'

'Really?' said Amos. 'I didn't know that. Who told you that?'

Of course it was a lie but it was for a good cause. I was only doing it to cheer Amos up.

Before I could expand on that lie, Amos said, 'Michigan is my home! I can't move away from there. You know I called about a volunteer job at my hospital back in Detroit?'

'Is that the same hospital you owe thousands of dollars to; the one you told me were sending you threatening letters to pay up or else?' I asked.

Amos nodded affirmatively. I tried to tell him that once they found out his name, they would never let him volunteer. I was also trying to get him to stay for selfish reasons. If he got a place in Berkeley, he would let me stay, since I was his only real friend. I told him that if he got a place here, we could go and meet women at Telegraph Avenue all the time and that he could also invite Miss Davis over for dinner.

I couldn't shake the con artist in me. My mother was always conning people, especially men. I remember riding across country with these strange men she had met in cafés. They would end up driving us all over the Midwest. When we got to where she wanted to go, she would get rid of them. Even when I was a teenager, I remember her meeting men at bars and going off with them for free drinks and dinner and then getting them to take her home thinking there would be sex involved. I remember many men beating on the door to get in. I assumed she hated men, since I'd never seen her being intimate with them in any way, even when she was hustling them for something. I asked myself how she'd got this way and thought about an incident I'd once witnessed.

I was staying with my mother once at my grandmother's and my mother had fallen asleep on the couch. My grandmother walked in and proceeded to jump all over her, saying the couch was too nice to use for sleeping. A few days later I saw my mom's drunken brother passed out on it and my grandmother didn't say a word. I knew that bothered my mother. I also knew she was used to it. On top of this I knew that my mother's second husband used to beat her all the time and literally tried to throw her out of a second-storey window. She had been abused by men all her life, in one way or another. I guess I'd just answered my own question.

My old man was a con man too. I guess the apple doesn't fall far from the tree. I had become better than them both.

To my mom's credit she was always working at one job or another. It was tough for her because she had no real education and was always in some sort of sales position. As far as my grandparents were concerned, all I got from them was a big nose and skinny legs! I mean, what were the chances of them both being that way? I was doomed from the start.

I continued trying to get Amos to stay in Berkeley, but he had his heart set on going back. I'm not sure why. As far as I knew, he had no friends. I knew he had a brother who was a chiropractor, but he had his own family to deal with. I finally gave up and tried to connect with him on what his friendship had meant to me.

'Hey, Amos, I'm really going to miss you. You're the man around here. It won't be the same without you.'

He thanked me.

'I know it's going to be a long cab ride to the airport tomorrow, Amos. I wonder what will be going through your mind.'

I knew Amos was terrified. I reflected back on that girl from Texas who was leaving the day I arrived. Her anxiety was a ten and her day was a zero. I remembered opening my big mouth about how her score should have been a nine or a ten and that she should have been excited about leaving here. I wish dearly I hadn't said that. I started to think about my time getting closer and any way I could find to con Jimmy or Tonya into letting me staying another month.

I shook hands with Amos and wished him the best. One thing I had in common with Amos: I would not sleep well that night.

FIGHT AT THE OK CORRAL

I felt really sad the next morning. Amos was my one true ally. I felt I could tell him anything. I mean, he always winked at me when I said my day was a two and my anxiety was an eight. He knew I was having a great time here with all the women I was involved with. He even told me once that I had no OCD symptoms whatsoever and I was living in a fantasy here.

He asked me to walk him to the taxi but I couldn't. It stems back to when I was younger. Whenever somebody positive came into my life, even for a short time, I couldn't bear saying goodbye. When they got ready to leave, I would mysteriously disappear somewhere and cry my eyes out.

Everyone thought I was just rude. I wanted to tell Amos my reasons but I couldn't.

Of course, I never really told anybody the true symptoms of my OCD, either. I mean, there was some hint of it in cognitive therapy but that was it. I was probably the only one here who was still a mystery.

I used Amos's departure as a way of putting off Tonya's trial by cereal until the next day. It wasn't that I was too anxious about it. I was just afraid that, if I passed it, Tonya might think I was ready to go home. That's really why I stalled the test.

I thought about this as I entered the men's group. I was really not in the mood for hearing anybody going on about themselves, let alone Po' White Trash, but I would play the model patient by putting in an appearance. I snuck in a cookie that I took from the kitchen table, but within minutes of eating it I'd nodded off into dream world. I didn't feel too guilty about falling asleep because I got absolutely nothing out of the group, though the instructor was a real nice man.

It wasn't long before someone was shaking me. It was the instructor, asking me why I was sleeping. I didn't want to get into an argument with him and just said I had no reason.

Po' White Trash yelled at me, 'Hey, don't those cookies taste like marijuana, James?'

Oh no, my secret was out! I wanted to kill Po' White. How did he know? I thought about what Alley had said about nothing really being a secret around here and how I'd probably given too many clues away in some of the therapy groups. I felt all eyes were on me. My mind started racing. Should I attack Po' White and get kicked out? Or, even worse, start asking this piece of shit for reassurance?

I needed to be cool and remember all that I had learned here. Realistically, there would be no pot in the cookies. If there was, everybody would be in big trouble; or I could take it a step further and remember something the Doc had told me: 'So what if there is pot or anything? What's the worst that can happen?'

Suddenly I felt a strange surge of confidence and said, 'I wish these cookies did have some pot in them!'

There was dead silence. I stared at Po' White and he stared back, waiting to see if I was going to attack him.

'Yeah, I could sure use a buzz right now,' Barney added unexpectedly.

To my surprise most everyone joined in with similar comments.

I was taken aback again when Dan, the instructor, said, 'James, you look high.'

Another jolt. I knew he was testing me. He must have been well aware of my problem too. Again I had another burst of confidence. It seemed like all the thousands of anxiety attacks I'd had in the past flashed before my eyes. Remembering how uncomfortable they made me feel gave me the confidence to say, 'I don't want any more of that crap!'

Before I knew it, Dan was saying class was dismissed. I ran for the computer. I knew Amos would have been proud. I had beaten Po' White without laying a hand on him. I would have to say if there were three steps in recovery, I had definitely taken the first two. I was looking forward to number three. I also had the fear that Dan would tell the Doc I was cured and they would send me home. All in all, though, it seemed like a good predicament.

HEMP

I took off for Telegraph Avenue first thing in the afternoon and walked up it looking for the gang. I spotted Kenny begging near his old spot and remembered my promise not to do any avoidance. I walked over to him and prepared for his verbal onslaught. He was ready for me.

'Hey, dude, I have to whisper. This whole area is wired, if you know what I mean.'

Of course I didn't know what he meant!

'CIA, dude. They got this whole street wired for sound. For both our protection, give me some money without my asking. I know they're trying to bust me for begging. We're going to cross them up, dude. When I mention the "Big Island", dude, that is the code word for you to lay some bread in my cup. That way they never hear me asking you for money. They can't bust me unless they hear me asking you for money. Hey, did I tell you I surfed the BIG ISLAND, dude?'

I looked on, bewildered.

'Hey, did I tell you I surfed the BIG ISLAND, DUDE?'

I didn't respond, as I wasn't sure what I was supposed to do. A moment later Kenny moved his cup and yelled right in my ear, 'Did I tell you I SURFED THE BIG ISLAND, DUDE?'

'Yes, now quit yelling at me!' I replied.

He moved the cup right under my chin. I threw a quarter into it, hoping that would shut him up. He smiled like the cat who just ate the canary. In his feeble mind he had just pulled one over on the CIA. I thought about telling him that if the CIA had him wired, they would have heard him telling me how he was going to cross them up. I guess I should have taken him home with me instead of Ray Ray. Of course, for him it would have been a one-way trip.

Kenny then spotted another student coming out of the

deli and zoomed after her. I watched in amazement as the young girl, probably a Berkeley student, gave him her sandwich and conversed with him as he devoured it. I decided I'd had enough of Kenny for the day and made my way over to the Park.

I saw a young hippy sitting by himself. I had made up my mind to try to stay focused today and forget about the girls. I sat down next to him. He was putting on some kind of lotion from a tube.

'Hey, try some of this hemp, dude, it's really good stuff,' he said.

Hemp! I knew that had something to do with marijuana. I asked the guy where he'd got the tube and he said some girl had bought it down at the bath shop on the corner.

I freaked out as I watched him spreading it all over his face. A moment later he offered me the tube. I reluctantly backed out. I started reassuring myself a little. I started thinking things like, 'If it got you high, they wouldn't be able to sell it. It was in a container so it had to be legit.' I finally built up the nerve to ask the guy if I could look at the bottle. I held it in my hands as the anxiety built.

I started having thoughts about Woody Harrelson and how he was always getting arrested for advocating the use of hemp. I rolled the tube around in my hands for a while until I got the nerve to squeeze a small amount onto my thumb. I was feeling pretty good about myself until the clown remarked, 'I get a buzz just rubbing it on my hands!'

I started to panic. I tried to calm down and reassure myself with cognitive therapy. 'Always ask yourself where the proof is. Slow down and ask yourself, is it logical to have this fear?' To my chagrin, it didn't work this time.

I immediately ran down to the bath shop to check it out. I walked in and asked if they had any hemp products. The girl working there took me over to an aisle full of hemp oils and lotions. I slowly picked up a bottle like the young hippy's and read the label. I knew I was looking for reassurance as I read the ingredients. Of course, I was petrified that I might find: 'Use at your own risk, can cause you to get high!' Needless to say, this wasn't to be found.

I tried to make up for reading the label by spraying some of the hemp oil on my hands. That bothered me some, but not enough. Bingo! I spotted the mother lode. There was a tube that read 'Hemp Lip Balm'. Putting a little on my hands was one thing, but putting some on my mouth was a whole different animal.

I opened the cap but that was as far as I would go. I needed stimulation. The only salesgirl in the place was fat and unattractive. More importantly she wasn't Asian. Nevertheless, I kept telling myself that if I wanted to get well, I had to make sacrifices. I approached the girl.

'Hey, do you have any Japanese or Asian in you?'

The girl looked bewildered by that question.

I quickly covered my tracks. 'You know, the Japanese are the smartest people on the planet. I mean, look at Berkeley; it's full of Japanese people. That's why I was hoping you had some Japanese in you.'

I quickly put the lip balm on the counter to pay for it. I'm not sure why, but the flirting worked for me. And for the girl? Well, you know the answer. I decided I had done enough just in buying the balm and would not try using it until later in the week. The girl looked relieved when I left.

AN ALL-TIME LOW

I hurried to catch the bus. I made a vow on the way back to stop talking to all these women. It was ridiculous, a man my age acting like some kid in junior high. It boggled my mind why these girls talked to me, let alone joined me for lunch or coffee. I'm not good looking, at least not in the classical sense. Maybe they thought I was funny. I hoped it wasn't because they felt sorry for me. As I stepped onto the bus, I thought of a way of curing myself.

I looked around and spotted a guy close to my age – my real age, not the one I had been lying about for years. I concluded that he was about as good looking as me. I then looked around the bus for a young, attractive woman. I spotted one and tried to imagine this man going over and hitting on her, for lack of a better term. As much as I wanted to see a pretty picture, it just wouldn't fly! Looking at it from her perspective, why would she want some old fart when she could get a young, virile man who didn't have wrinkles and crow's feet? Yes, I was beginning to see the light for the first time. Maybe this would push me into reality. I smiled as I got off the bus.

I looked at my watch and realised I still had a bit of time before the last group of the day. I went into the doughnut shop and got a Dr Pepper – thank God, one of few places in Berkeley that had it – and chilled out in there, reading a paper. I was minding my own business when this creature walked by and sat right across from my table. She was stunning. She had a unique look, like a mixture of Asian and Spanish. I was just about to say hello when I remembered my promise. No more women! She looked up and smiled at me; it was over.

'Say, where are you from? I noticed an accent when you got your coffee,' I said.

Of course, that was BS. I'd only noticed her when she'd walked by.

'Hot chocolate,' she said. 'I don't drink coffee.'

'Wow, really? I'm the same way. Give me hot chocolate or nothing!'

She looked straight at my soft drink as if to say 'that doesn't look like hot chocolate to me'.

'Oh, I have a stomach ache, and these carbonated drinks help me out.'

She nodded, unconvinced.

'So, where are you from?' I said again.

'I'm from New Mexico, near Albuquerque.'

'Wow, me too! I'm from Albuquerque. Grew up right by the airport. So what brought you here to Berkeley?'

She told me she'd got a job here working for an airline. That made sense to me; this beauty would make a great stewardess. I couldn't keep from staring. She had this incredibly intense look, as if her face was meant to be photographed.

'Hey, you're staring at me,' she said.

'Oh, I'm sorry. James Bailey, looking at you.'

'I'm Lupi. So, James Bailey, what kind of work do you think I do for the airlines?'

I said stewardess. She shook her head. I continued going down the list from ticket agent to public relations but kept getting the no sign. I finally gave up.

'I'm an airplane mechanic!'

My heart dropped. Red flags were shooting in my mind like fireworks! Why couldn't I be some pig farmer from North Dakota or some corn shucker from Nebraska or just a guy from Louisiana who never went to New Orleans? Then, what she had just said would have meant nothing! I could have replied, 'Great. I'm glad a beautiful, sexy, exotic woman like you is a mechanic.'

But no, I had lived in places like LA, which had jaded me, and I knew what worldly people knew. 'You're gay, aren't you?' I said.

'Yes, I am. How did you know?'

'Well, I'm gay too, and it takes one to know one. Do you mind if I join you?'

Of course, she gladly invited me over. I began by asking her if she was in a relationship and she told me she had only just moved here and didn't know anyone. She asked me if I had a lover.

'No,' I replied. 'I've been doing a lot of soul-searching lately and I just feel empty with my male lovers. I think it's finally hitting me that maybe I would really like a family. I'm seriously thinking about giving women a try. I mean, life passes you by. You know what I mean?'

'I understand what you're saying. I've thought about it too.'

I was in heaven. Yes, I could change this beautiful woman. I could understand her like no other man. Why? Because I always rented lesbian porno.

'Of course, I only thought about changing in high school. Now I would never consider a man!' she said.

I felt like a bolt of lightning had hit me.

'You know, James, I have a friend and he's just the sweetest guy I know. He just broke up with his boyfriend and you would be perfect for him!'

I got up and slowly walked towards the exit. Even in my dazed state, I realised that I'd hit an all-time low.

ATONEMENT

Lisa seemed to get better about her hands one day and then relapse again the next. I didn't get to know her as well as I wanted to because she was only a day patient. She had an apartment close to the hospital. The last group of the day had just begun when Lisa had another anxiety attack. I had seen another girl enter the bathroom and she was known to stay in there a long time, dealing with her rituals. So I knew Lisa couldn't get into the bathroom even if they let her.

'I need to wash my hands because this chair is crawling with germs,' said Lisa as she jumped out of her chair.

'Lisa, there are no germs on the chair,' said Mary.

'James, are there germs on that chair?' said Lisa.

Oh boy. I was on the spot again. I could say no. Of course, that would lead to Lisa saying, 'Then why are you afraid to touch it, James?'

'Lisa, you are disrupting group,' said Mary.

Here was my chance for atonement. I knew there were no germs on that chair but I still had that 'there must be something wrong with it if she's afraid of it' feeling. I thought about all the things I was doing at Telegraph. This was mere child's play compared to that. I grabbed the chair and rubbed my hands all over it!

'See, Lisa, there's nothing wrong with your chair.'

Lisa thanked me and sat down. Of course, all I'd done was to give her reassurance. But that said, I felt good about myself. Temporarily.

WHAT A GUY

I worried a bit before breakfast the next day. I knew that Tonya would be coming to lay the acid test, so to speak, on me. That said, I wondered how I'd slept so soundly. I knew if I was back in Louisiana and the doctor there had proposed the same idea, I wouldn't even have considered it.

Then again, he would never have considered it, if for no other reason than to protect himself from my obsessing. 'What made you think of doing this, doc? Would you really put something in my cereal?' I would have asked him that question at least 50 times. He would have had to say, 'I wouldn't do that to you!' Of course, I would then say, 'Did you say "would" or "would not"?' After endless reassurances I would finally wear him out until he would literally beg me to leave. The secretary there had been well aware of my behaviour and was instructed to keep me from getting back into the doctor's quarters once I'd exited. My only option was to wait all day at the parking lot for the doc to get off work. The doc had learned, for his self-preservation, to proceed with caution in our sessions. And this worked fine for both of us. He did me so much good while I was there that really he was a big step on my road to recovery.

I should have been elated that I'd now reached a stage where I could face this test without my anxiety hitting the ceiling. That's how a normal person would have felt. But I wasn't normal – and I hadn't been even before I'd got the OCD. I did want to get better, but just not so fast. I was having a ball at Berkeley. And that reminded me, I'd wanted to email a new girl I'd met on Telegraph before Tonya came in, so I quickly ran to the computer.

To my dismay the big guy was on it. He was looking up some rap crap and listening to it on the headphones. I wanted to tell him to get off, but I'd almost got in big trouble before doing that. I had to try another tack.

'Hey, big guy, you know my friend Ray Ray was asking me about you. She said you were cute and wondered if you were in a serious relationship.'

It was hard keeping a straight face.

'She really asked about me?' he said.

I nodded.

'What about you? I thought you liked her.'

'You know I'm only into Asian and Hispanic women.'

'I thought she was Hispanic.'

Well, the big guy had a point. I had bragged that she was Hispanic and had been delighted when people like Tonya called her Jennifer Lopez. I had to think quickly.

'Well, to be honest I found out that only her mother is Hispanic, and, as you know from our therapy groups, one of my OCD obsessions is that everything has to be full. Ever since I found out she was only half, well, I end up having an anxiety attack every time I try to call her!'

'Wow,' said the big guy. 'How did she take the news?'

'I didn't want to hurt her feelings, so I never told her. But I was hoping you would let me email her and set you up. Of course, with my OCD it might take hours or even days before I finish writing to her about you.'

The big guy jumped up and told me to get on the computer and that any time I needed to get on, I should just let him know. 'James, I was wrong about you. You're a real nice guy!'

Hey, I did the guy a favour. He would do something constructive with all his free time instead of wasting it on rap music and mindless computer games. I also knew my guilt would kick in later and I would find him a girl to go out with somewhere on Telegraph. Deep down I was very sensitive, but I had to hide it at all costs.

THE ACID TEST

I heard Tonya calling my name just as I finished my emails. She took me into the dining room where everybody was having breakfast and asked me to sit down. I told her there was no way I would do the experiment with any patients or counsellors in the room. I figured the counsellors knew just about everybody's OCD but mine, since I was almost always on my own when I went to Telegraph Avenue.

I also knew Dorwina couldn't have known, because she would have used it against me. I knew I had to get stronger and stronger because it was just a matter of time before she found out. That would be the ultimate acid test! If I could stand her throwing innuendos about my OCD, I could make it for sure in the outside world. It also crossed my mind that I might be getting obsessed with Dorwina, maybe even paranoid, because Dorwina, though not caring for my attitude, wouldn't do anything to jeopardise her job. I quickly dismissed that as Tonya cleared the room for our experiment.

I waited anxiously as she left for the kitchen to get whatever I was supposed to eat. A moment later she returned with a bowl of what looked like Rice Krispies and set it down before me. I grabbed the spoon and held onto it, waiting for her to say something. I looked at her and she looked at me for what seemed like an eternity. I finally broke the silence by asking her if there was anything in the cereal.

'I'm not going to tell you that, James.'

I didn't know what to do. I finally told her I wasn't going to eat it unless she told me what was in it.

'There's a pot-pourri of things: a little acid, a little cocaine and a little ex. Don't worry, though, I put just a very small amount in so you won't freak out!'

Wow, she was good. I impulsively took a big spoonful of cereal and started eating it as fast as I could, whispering to myself all along. Tonya looked on flabbergasted as I continued to eat.

'James, what is that you're whispering?'

I blurted out, 'You would never do anything to hurt me. It would not only be illegal but immoral!'

She told me there was a little heroin in the cereal, too.

I continued, 'You would never do anything to hurt me. It would be illegal and immoral!'

Tonya got up and walked out of the room in frustration. I finished off the cereal. I was not as confident as I'd led Tonya to believe. I was trying to figure out if I'd done the right thing with Tonya. She could tell the Doc I was cured and send me home. Or she could say I was hiding behind the words I was whispering.

I told myself I wanted to stay for the food and the women. But deep down, I liked the safety net of having people around 24 hours a day to help me. I was confused about how I really felt. I tried to console myself by saying, 'No matter how long I get to stay, whether a month or even two, a day will come when I have to leave, just like everybody else. That's reality, cured or not!'

TONYA TAKES A TRIP

Tonya was so agitated by my antics that she was beside herself. I decided to get away from her, since the experiment was over. Although she told me to stop repeating the words, I just said them in my mind. Was the experiment a success? In my mind, yes – I did eat the cereal!

I decided to bop down to Telegraph Avenue a little early. Just as I opened the front door, Tonya accosted me.

'James, I've decided to go with you to Telegraph Avenue today.'

Oh, great. What was I to do? I knew she was getting back at me for the way I'd got around the test. I panicked and said,

'Well, I really don't need any help. Maybe it would be better to help Barney or somebody who can't go on their own.'

There was a long pause. I knew that was a stupid thing to say. I was a self-confessed con man. That said, anyone who took psychology for beginners would know that.

'No, James. I feel like I've been neglecting you for other patients. We can go in my car and be back for lunch.'

I had no choice. Reluctantly I walked with her to her car, wondering what would happen if Ray Ray or any of my Asian women spotted me and came up and asked about me, about my research and how I had missed them for coffee and blah, blah, blah . . .

On the trip to Telegraph I thought that maybe warming up to her might be the best route to take. I asked her about her family. I had seen her husband and kids at the Christmas party.

'James, let's stick to the business at hand.'

I must say I was a little taken aback by her comment. Amos had told me she was a bit cold, even though she was not his behaviour therapist. Apparently he had been in the middle of several conversations and she'd happened to walk by, going to her office, and said to him that he was obsessing. Of course, he probably was.

Then again, as I've said, you can't ask a question without the staff accusing you of asking for reassurance. I had once asked one of the male counsellors to open up the bathroom next to my room so I could take a shower. He asked me why I didn't use the shower on the other side of the hallway. I told him it was easier to use the one right next to my room. He accused me of avoiding the other one. I finally said, 'Why in the hell would anyone want to walk all the way to the other side when there's a bathroom right next to their room? What the hell has that got to do with OCD? Any rational person would want to use the bathroom closest to their room!'

He disagreed and said I was afraid of germs or something. To be honest I was hiding the fact that I'd stashed laxatives in my drawer. The rules said you couldn't have anything in your room that had to do with medication. If they'd caught me crossing the corridor with a glass of water from the bathroom they'd have wanted to know why. But I didn't think I was doing anything wrong. I just wasn't prepared to go downstairs to Dorwina or any other counsellor every time I needed something to make me take a crap.

I snapped out of my daydream as Tonya offered to buy me some coffee after she'd parked the car. I was praying she wouldn't go in the academic bookstore. As we walked down the street, I spotted Jazz begging. He waved at me. As we passed him, I couldn't help myself and called out to Tonya, 'Still going to buy me breakfast, honey?'

Tonya, a little befuddled, said, 'OK.'

Jazz smiled from ear to ear. He thought I was hustling this girl for food. She asked me who he was. I told her he was one of the punks who unknowingly had been helping me out. She was proud of me for that.

I began to sweat as lots of Asian girls walked past me. I could just hear one of them saying something like, 'Hey, James, I enjoyed lunch the other day and, by the way, how is your documentary going?'

Luckily Tonya got a call on her cell phone. She acted like I was yesterday's news and said we had to get back to the house. I tried asking her what was wrong, but she ignored me. I thought back to when the Doc had told me she was my BT. I'd started asking for reassurance and wondered if she had a good track record. The Doc told me she had worked with hundreds of patients and been here longer than anyone. But Teddy Bear's BT, who was the best-looking one at Within Reach, later contradicted this good impression somewhat by saying to me, 'She's the only behaviour therapist here without a Doctorate.'

When we got back, I found out that the emergency was her husband had banged his toe or something. Of course, I was the guy who hadn't wanted Tonya to come with me, but now it bothered me that she had dismissed me for something so minor. I guess I was just looking for reassurance. I wanted Tonya to show me that she really liked me and I could count on her at any time for anything. In reality every therapist has to keep that distance and not cross that fine line. I guess I wanted her to cross it.

FINANCES

The last group started off as usual until it got to Ralph. Mary asked him to talk about his day and he proceeded to say his day was a three and his anxiety was a ten.

'It's my finances; they're killing me. I need to get my finances straight, uh, could I be excused? I need to make a phone call to get my finances straight.'

Mary politely said no.

He went off on a tirade. 'I don't like being treated like a child. I have finances I have to take care of. I paid good money to come here and I won't be treated like this!'

Barney then yelled out, 'You tell 'em, Ralph!'

Everybody broke into laughter.

I said, 'Hey, Ralph, there's a penny stuck in my chair. Could you get it out for me?'

Mary was beside herself. To be honest I thought she brought some of it on herself. She was never strict enough with us, especially with Barney. He'd say the stupidest things and Mary would just laugh and tell him to quiet down. Finally things got back under control. Mary told me it was my turn to give my scores.

As I began to speak, Barney jumped in with, 'Hey, we never got to give Ralph any feedback.'

Mary was outraged, but she knew this was one of the rules of this group. She reluctantly gave in and asked if anybody had any feedback for Ralph. I was the first one to open my mouth, 'cause I knew Barney was going to say something.

'Hey, Ralph,' I said. 'Some bank called for you and left a message for you to call. I wrote the number on the chalkboard but I noticed somebody must have erased it because it isn't there any more.'

Ralph leaped out of his chair and said, 'Oh no, did I write a bad cheque? Daddy will be mad!'

Barney jumped in and said, 'Bad cheques, Ralph. I'd hate to see you go to jail.' He pulled out his wallet and said, 'I got a twenty, Ralph, if it will help.'

Chaos broke out again as Ralph stood up and began pacing the floor. Of course, I had made all that up. Poor Ralph was about to have a nervous breakdown. We all got to laughing so loud that Mary threatened to call hospital security. Barney continued to make jokes about finances. I knew he would. Unlike me he couldn't control it. I also knew if he got kicked out I would be all alone on an island. Dorwina and the powers that be would be on me the whole time. He was my buffer. I finally got him to calm down.

Maybe Mary would forget the whole thing. Yeah, it was Friday and all this would blow over during the weekend.

Maybe.

AN ANGEL FROM OSAKA

I'd headed back down to San Francisco again one day and was waiting for the BART to take me back when I stumbled on possibly the sweetest girl I have ever met. She, of course, was young and Japanese. Her name was Yuki. She had come to California from Osaka to study English. Now, she wasn't your classic beauty like the rich girl from Tokyo, but she was cute.

I proceeded to lay all my lines on her and she just smiled. She knew I had never been to Japan and was full of it but she sat and talked with me like we were old friends. I was running out of time, so I invited her to ride the BART with me. She was meant to be going the other way, but she climbed on board with me anyway – not because she was naive, but because she was sweet and kind and sensed how lonely I really was, under my display of bravado. She even got off at my stop in Berkeley and caught the bus with me all the way to my last stop, the doughnut shop.

I tried to give her back her bus fare but she refused. We started seeing each other pretty regularly after that. We would meet at Market Street in San Fran or she would catch the bus to meet me at the doughnut shop. I would try to scare her off by bragging about my past sexual exploits but she never even flinched. All too soon she had to go back home to Japan, where she had a boyfriend waiting. He was one lucky guy.

CAUGHT ON THE HOT SEAT

I was excited when I got up on Saturday. We had one group meeting in the morning: the usual one dealing with exposures. Anna told me she wanted to catch the bus with me after class to Telegraph. She was a nice person, but I didn't want to deal with her constant chatter. I told her I hoped I would run into some of my homeless friends on the way and she freaked and made up some story that she had to wait for her boyfriend to call.

I knew she would weenie out. I didn't understand her. Why come all this way and then not really try to get better? I knew if I was running this place, I would develop some kind of plan to make patients confront their fears the way I had. If I had an impulse that forced extreme guilt on me, causing me to take risks that made me better, other people must have had something inside of them to push their buttons. But Within Reach couldn't do this for them; the counsellors could only lead us to our exposures, and the rest had to come from within. I knew I was lucky that I'd found my catalyst by pure chance. I'd improved more quickly than most, but even I wasn't strong enough to abandon my safety net forever and declare that I was never coming back. The place was a revolving door: a constant cycle of patients leaving and returning.

There were other people who'd recovered here. I'd heard about some girl who had been cured of pulling her hair. And, of course, there was Amos. The guys who played basketball all told me they still had numerous problems, though. Maybe I should open up a clinic myself. I had come to the conclusion that the only way to cure most of the severe OCD patients would be to make them sign some kind of consent that you could use the necessary force to push their buttons when needed.

This idea came to me as I was trying to help this patient from India. His father had come to America to visit him and was outside, honking, as they had plans for dinner. Ali wouldn't open the door until he got this feeling somewhere in his brain that it was safe to do so. Meanwhile his dad honked and honked. I yelled at Ali to open the fricking door. He refused. I finally grabbed his hand and stuck it on the knob to open it. He ended up cussing me out so I left him alone. Meanwhile his dad kept honking! Fifteen minutes later he finally got the feeling and opened the door.

In my imaginary clinic I'd be allowed to force people's hands onto doorknobs, or drag people out of the toilet if they were in there too long. I suppose it was just as well this place didn't exist. On a lighter note any clinic of mine would be fully staffed by ethnic minorities: say 80 per cent Asian and 20 per cent Hispanic. My bias against Caucasian women had grown and grown over the years. Only true Christian white women treated me like I was a human being. Maybe I should get to know some black women, too. I liked Alley a lot. Of course, she was probably gay. She was also mysterious. I would always see her leaving by herself. I also would bet money she was the only black girl in the world named Alley. That intrigued me too. I'm demented, and stuff like that intrigues me. Oh well, Alley would have to wait for another day.

I made my way down to the bus stop. I was supposed to come back for an afternoon class called Leisure Learning. I hated that class because the counsellor would encourage all the patients to go out and do something for the weekend like go to Telegraph Avenue or go out to dinner somewhere. All these people made these big plans and not many besides me ever left the fricking house! Why should I have to catch the bus all the way back for such nonsense?

The sun was shining and I was feeling good. I climbed on the bus and sat behind a white girl I had been chatting with on numerous occasions. She'd told me she had an apartment in the Elmwood district, a nice area of Berkeley and the home of Triumph. I was hoping that maybe if we became friends she might let me stay with her in the future. She had a black girl sitting next to her but this girl had a hat on and was reading a book, so I assumed they didn't know each other.

I was caught off guard when the white girl – Mandy or Mary or whatever her name was – turned and said, 'I saw you at Triumph Hospital yesterday. You were coming out of Within Reach.'

Man, I froze like a popsicle. Of course, I could fool Ray Ray – she was Mexican. But this was another matter. I impulsively said, 'Well, I'm a part-time counsellor there. How do you know about . . .?'

'What's up, James?'

I was shocked to see Alley staring at me. She was the girl with the hat on. I was always quick on my feet, but this time I was trapped. What could I say to get out of this?

Alley spoke casually. 'We were patients together, Mary and I, the last time I was here.'

Wow, I knew that Mary was a little off-centre, but what were the odds she would have OCD too?!

I knew Alley liked me, so I chanced my arm with: 'Yes, I've been helping Alley with her problems. She has come a long way since you two were at Triumph.'

I winked at Alley and she just smiled. I came to the realisations that I wouldn't be staying with this girl, Mary, and that Alley was out of my reach – not because she might be gay, but because she was good and kind: far removed from me.

SANITY/INSANITY

One thing kept going over and over in our brains. Everyone here kept telling us we weren't crazy. I think most of us found that hard to believe. I mean, Teddy flushed the toilet and went back a hundred times to make sure he'd flushed it. Was that normal? Anna thought that by touching someone or something she would be stricken with Aids and die. Ralph would . . . well, I'm not sure what Ralph's deal was exactly. I only knew he had a thing about finances and being on the phone. Amos had repeated the same thing over and over again with the same enthusiasm. Po' White had to count all the steps he took, and if he lost count he had to start over. Me: I had to ask reassurance over and over again to be convinced that nobody had put drugs in my food. I had hallucinated all the way from LA to Louisiana without taking drugs and that can't be too normal. Or what about the girl from Jersey who was taking shock treatments? Or me again, needing a waitress to give me reassurance about the food to stop me from blowing my head off! Yes, we were all off-centre in some way.

Most of us could have mistakenly walked up the hill to the psychiatric ward of Triumph Hospital and no one working there would have known the difference. Yes, we had to be insane to some degree, didn't we? Most of us were on social security disability. I mean, it wasn't much money, but there is security even with a small amount of money. Of course, Dr Swenson never used the word crazy. It was all OCD. Whatever you did, it was OCD. I guess it sounds better than saying you're crazy, but it doesn't exactly sound great, does it? I can just imagine meeting some girl and having lunch with her and excusing myself about 20 times to go off and wash my hands: 'Sorry, honey, I got OCD and can't help myself.' That would be akin to saying, 'Yeah, I got the runs. I hope you don't mind if I get up every few minutes to take a crap.'

Are we crazy? I guess everybody has his or her own definition. I will say this: I've never had the desire to harm any of the girls I've ever met, even in my darkest moments. That I say in my own defence.

COLLEGE AVENUE

I was walking up Telegraph looking for women or exposures when I ran into Jazz and Rabbit. They were standing in front of the news-stand sharing a bottle of vodka. Rabbit had the ominous green briefcase right next to him. Jazz was drunk, as usual, and told me he'd got kicked out of somebody's place last night but he didn't know why or where. His face had green swastikas painted all over it. He said it was like that when he woke up. I don't think I've ever seen anybody look quite that bad before. If he lived another year, I would be shocked.

I sat down for a moment to rest near the briefcase when Rabbit spoke to me with authority. 'Squiggles don't want anybody near the briefcase.'

I replied casually, 'Squiggles runs a tight ship, huh?'

Jazz replied drunkenly, 'He thinks he does!'

Rabbit told Jazz to shut his big mouth. I wanted Jazz to tell me about the briefcase, but I didn't want him to get beaten up either. I told him I had bummed some change and said, 'Let's go get a beer.'

Of course, he happily agreed as he downed the last drop of vodka.

I really liked Jazz and Rage. I felt that, under different circumstances, they would have been fun to pal around with. I got Jazz a beer and started asking him about the mysterious green briefcase. He told me that Squiggles kept money and drugs in there. He also said he always had someone else watching it, because he had warrants out for his arrest and if he got busted he would be a three-time loser and thus get life in prison. Good old Squiggles. I had something to obsess about now, but this time I'd enjoy it: Squiggles!

Jazz ended up passing out, so I decided to go to College Avenue: an interesting place in Berkeley with lots of unique shops and restaurants. A girl from Osaka had warned me that all the Asian girls were talking about me around Telegraph, so I was making an effort to be a little more low-key.

I really wanted to visit Osaka some day for real. Yuki, who was kind and sweet to me, was from Osaka, and now so was the girl from Telegraph Avenue who'd warned me. Yes, someday I would go there.

I really wanted to enjoy this sunny day in College Avenue. I'd heard on the radio this was the warmest winter in the Bay Area in a hundred years. Hey, life is great, I was thinking as I made my way around the shops. When I'd been in them all at least twice, and seen no available women, I decided to do some exposures. I walked up to some homeless men, shook hands and asked them if there was a shelter around. I was almost obsessed with getting exposure, which was good.

I finally made my way down to a bookstore that had a balcony for coffee drinkers to read and study on. I saw this beautiful girl and approached her and was about to deliver my usual opening line: 'Studying hard?' Of course, the next line would have been, 'What's your major?' Or if she'd been reading a novel I'd have said, 'Is the book any good?' You get the picture.

As I opened my mouth, the girl said, 'Hey, James, how's your documentary coming?'

My goodness, it was a Chinese girl I had met at the academic bookstore. Again with the documentary! Once again I had to make adjustments to my lies.

'I'm just a writer doing research on the homeless.'

I felt a little uncomfortable with her because she kept talking about the documentary. I decided I'd better make my way back home, since it was my turn to do the clean-up.

I left and was making my way back to Telegraph and the bus stop. As luck would have it, I passed an Asian girl waiting on a street corner along the way. I looked her over and decided she was my favourite, Japanese, and said, 'Say, what kind of Asian are you? I bet money you're my favourite: Japanese, right?'

'Yeah. So?' she said.

'Well, I got to tell you, the Japanese are the Rolls-Royce of the Asian population. Y'all are so smart and so kind that I find myself only attracted to Japanese women.'

'You're a racist, and I prefer you don't talk to me any more!' she said as she quickly walked away.

I was shocked. What had I said? I was very kind to her. Maybe she was gay. Still, it did bother me. I walked down to catch the bus and spotted the 'mystery girl' Alley coming from the other direction. I tried to get her to tell me where she always disappeared to but she just changed the subject.

'How many women did you meet today, James, and why in the hell are you wearing two different kinds of shoes?'

I'd forgotten I had done that. I had my reasons. 'Hey, my theory is that only an interesting girl will notice that I have two different shoes on. Of course, she will be compelled to come up to me to ask me why. Thus, a conversation has started.'

'You're so full of it, James!'

'Hey, it worked. You're an interesting girl.'

Alley just gave me a smirk.

'I think I got a thing for you, Alley.'

Alley's face turned green. I was only joking around but somewhere deep in her psyche I had pushed a panic button. I tried to laugh it off but she got very quiet. I had a funny feeling that our friendship or whatever it was would never be the same. On reflection, though, maybe I wasn't joking. She was the only person there who seemed to accept me faults and all. She always stood up for me even when I was wrong, which was most of the time.

We got off the bus and walked up the hill to Within Reach without saying a word. I tried to equate it to the feeling of loss I had when Amos left. This was different. Maybe I had fallen in love with Alley. I did the only thing I knew how to do. I got on the computer and started emailing my Asian girls.

TEDDY BEAR GOES HOME

I had talked to the Doc about Teddy trying new medicine and he'd agreed. On my encouragement, Teddy Bear had then gone to see him about it. He'd been given a new prescription but the result was the same: extreme anxiety.

Teddy told me at the last outing that he wanted to go home. He was crying. I'd never seen him showing much emotion before that, so he really had to be suffering. I tried to talk him out of it, but ended up having an anxiety attack myself. He made a remark to me that he was hoarding some of his drugs. He said he was afraid of getting hooked on them. Then he offered me a mint. Since I was trying to keep exposing myself, I took it. A moment later I started thinking he'd given me one of his drugs instead. I mean, my thinking was, it's possible because he could have kept them all in the same box.

I reluctantly said to him, 'Hey, that was a mint you gave me, right?'

'Yeah, I think so. Why, doesn't it taste like a mint?'

My mind was off and running again! I was in survival mode. I couldn't care less if Teddy Bear left or stayed. Hell, I couldn't care less if he lived or died at that moment. That's how strong my anxiety attacks were. Only people who have them would understand what I'm saying. What could I ask him now for reassurance? Again the therapy kicked in. I remembered him saying, 'Why, doesn't it taste like a mint?'

I rolled my tongue and tasted the minty taste. I reasoned I'd never tasted a prescription drug that tasted like a mint. Hell, they all tasted bitter.

'Hey, guy, you got another mint?'

Though I attacked my anxiety head on, which I felt great about, I was too drained to muster much of a pep talk for Teddy staying.

A week later he was packing.

'I'm going to miss you, Teddy Bear. I wish you would reconsider.'

'James, it was kind of mutual between me and the house. I've been missing classes too.'

The poor guy was shaking like a leaf. I searched for something profound to say, but nothing came to me. I hugged him and said, 'Hey, Teddy Bear, I won't have anybody to talk to about the Rangers.'

He smiled brighter than ever before.

THE WARNING

I knew something was up on Monday morning as I waited for the first group to start. Miss Hines, the head honcho, was there and so was every other counsellor. Someone yelled out that I had a phone call and Miss Hines reminded me that the group would start in three minutes and I wasn't to be late.

I ran up the stairs to see who would be calling me this close to group. My brother knew not to call before group. I answered the phone and was excited to find out it was Teddy Bear. He had left just yesterday. I was really touched that he'd asked for me. Although he didn't say much – he wasn't capable of that – he had called and asked for me. I felt good.

That feeling didn't last long. The group started out with a bang. Miss Hines stood up and spoke to all of us.

'I have been getting all kinds of reports of people disrupting groups and, even worse than that, singling out certain patients and laughing at them!'

She looked right at Barney and me. I knew she was talking about our behaviour towards Ralph and Linzy. How could a person not laugh when Ralph was going on about his finances? It was hysterical. Besides, we weren't really laughing at him; it was more 'laughing at the situation'.

Linzy was another case. She obviously had a lot more problems than OCD, but no one seemed to want to deal with that. I stayed on her back about how she would just sit and stare at the radio. I had reported her to numerous counsellors who literally had to get two or three people to pull her away from it.

Miss Hines brought me back to reality.

'We have literally hundreds of people waiting to get into this place. In all my years here I have never seen a bunch of patients act like this! You're not children, and I advise you to quit acting that way or you will be gone! That bed of yours is waiting to be filled. You'd better realise you came here to get well. So shape up or ship out! It's your choice. If I have any more complaints, heads will roll around here. Do I make myself clear?'

Everybody shook his or her head in agreement. Even Barney, who always had to add something, was quiet. Ralph didn't react in any way. Good ole Ralph. He didn't know he was the object of our impermissible laughter. Linzy didn't either. She was looking around the room for something to stare at.

The next group was very quiet. Of course, Miss Hines sat in.

I finished the group and walked over to Dr Swenson's office. I knocked and walked in.

'So what's up?' asked Dr Swenson.

'Hey, Doc, I ate a sandwich this homeless heroin addict gave me.'

'Did you get high from it, James? Because a lot of the crack heroin they smoke these days gets all over everything.'

My anxiety shot up like one of those Roman candles you see on the Fourth of July. I knew he was baiting me, but I still had the anxiety. I was pondering what to say when he did me a favour and changed the subject.

'I hear you and Jerry haven't been getting along.'

'Who in the hell is he?' I asked.

He told me I had told him off in men's group.

'Oh, Po' White Trash. Hell, I like him. You remember I told you I always feel better when the sun is shining and that the sun is my only friend and that the sun is God to me? Well, his teeth are so yellow, every time I look at him I feel I'm basking in the sun!'

The Doc had a nervous smile. I knew I could get away

with this a tad because Po' White had another doctor, so the only time my doc came into contact with Po' White was at basketball. The Doc regained his composure and told me I had to try to get along with people.

'Am I close to getting kicked out, Doc?'

'No, you won't get kicked out.'

I told him that Tonya and Jimmy had said that I might get to stay for four months instead of three. He asked me why I was so obsessed with four. I couldn't tell him that I was having the time of my life, girls included!

'I just think if I stay for four I would have much more confidence in making it on the outside.'

He disagreed. I finally gave in and said, 'In the big picture, Doc, I am better now than ever before. It's almost amazing the transformation I have made!'

He told me great and also said the only way you can make it after you leave the programme is to develop an after-care programme.

'Volunteer until you get enough confidence to try and get a part-time job,' said Dr Swenson. He also guaranteed me that I would 'totally relapse' if I didn't do an after-care programme. Of course, the Doc didn't know I wasn't your ordinary patient, and I was getting better mostly by myself thanks to all the Asian girls and the homeless at Telegraph. He caught me off guard when he said, 'I hope you've got the women thing under control. I have in my notes that you're emailing a lot of women.'

That damn Dorwina was hanging around the computer when I was talking to Barney about all of my emails. Of course, I was bragging to everyone about all the women I had met, so I had to take some of the blame.

'No, Doc. Those were some old emails from the past and a few I collected on Sunday on our outing.'

The Doc looked at me, unsure. I certainly couldn't tell him the truth about how I was leading a triple life at Telegraph Avenue.

'Hey, Doc, will I always have these thoughts? You know, like when you mentioned the heroin? And no, I'm not asking for reassurance.'

The Doc got serious, which really wasn't his bag. I mean, he would tell you something profound but he would always end it with a chuckle or a smile. Maybe that was his thing. But this time he was dead serious, so I listened intently.

'You will always get that "what if" feeling. There's no cure for obsessive-compulsive disorder. If you're lucky, and work hard like you have been doing, you can control maybe eighty per cent of it.'

I wasn't buying that. I had come so far, I knew if I really kept at it I could get more than that. I started to tell the Doc about Squiggles and my gang but it seemed so unreal that I decided to pass.

'Do you have any plans when you leave here, James?'

'You know, Doc, I live in this small town and just about every day a train comes through blocking traffic. I always imagine me jumping out of my car and hopping that freight. I would just love waving at all those people waiting in their cars as my train moved away. Of course, they would look at me like I was crazy but deep down, behind their little jobs and their security, they would know I was something they would never be: I was free!'

The Doc stared at me a moment before speaking. 'I can see why Mel Brooks likes you.'

'You're the man, Doc!'

And he was.

DORWINA'S REVENGE

It dawned on me as I got ready for my exposure that I had planned to ask the good Doc about taking a Valium once in a while. I felt I didn't need it now. I guess that is why Dr Swenson had been on that TV programme. He was good!

I walked around feeling good until I got the bad news that Dorwina was taking me and Po' White to Telegraph Avenue to supervise us. Man, I went from the penthouse to the outhouse in a matter of minutes. I knew Dorwina was still out to get me. Of course, my popping off to her all the time didn't help. I was also sure that reporting that email thing to the Doc wouldn't have been enough to satisfy her.

I jumped into the very last seat in the van. My luck got even worse when the big guy climbed in next to Po' White. This was going to be a long ride. It was same ol' same ol' as Po' White was telling the big guy about how Mary was so attracted to him. Oh, man, I had to hold my mouth to keep from laughing!

Mary was a beautiful blonde sex-pot who could have any guy in the world and certainly wouldn't go for this complete no-hoper. She also was probably the nicest counsellor there, even though she'd turned me in for smarting off to her and calling her a scatterbrain. To be honest that was my fault.

Just when I thought it couldn't get worse, Dorwina climbed into the van and turned up this rock station full blast. I tried yelling for her to turn it down but she ignored me. I tried to think positively and told myself that, with all the noise, I wouldn't hear those two clowns talking about how the counsellors had crushes on them.

Soon we were pulling up to Telegraph Avenue and parking. I knew I had to be super-careful today because Dorwina would love to report that I was chatting with women during my exposure. I also knew my way around Telegraph and the Park and would easily lose her.

'I want you to come with me, James,' she said.

'Well, I pretty much do my exposures on my own,' I quickly added.

'Not today.'

I had to come up with something fast.

'I thought I heard the Doc say he [I pointed at Po' White Trash, because I still couldn't remember his name] needs supervision today.'

Of course, the Doc hadn't said that. He wasn't even Po' White's physician. But Po' White and his buddy took the bait like I knew they would. A girl that looked like Dorwina wouldn't give them the time of day on the outside and, deep down, they knew that.

'Yeah, I need someone around. I get too anxious,' said Po' White.

The big guy said the same thing. They didn't want to be alone. Before I knew it I was on my way, solo. I heard Dorwina call out that I should rejoin them in front of the academic bookstore at a certain time so I waved OK.

I knew I had to stay away from any women so I did my usual and went in to get some hemp samples for my skin. I had finally started putting the lip balm on, and to my surprise it didn't give me much anxiety. I rubbed the oil on my face and started over to the front to say hi to the cashier. To my surprise she snuck into the back before I could reach her. She must have thought I had the hots for her from going in there all the time. Of course, I had been trying to be nice by telling her she was attractive. I should have been hurt. I guess that's what I get for flirting with a whale. Oh well.

I went back outside. I looked around suspiciously, not wanting to see Dorwina or Squiggles. I walked around touching garbage cans and shook hands with a few homeless men. I bummed a smoke and lit it up to blend in. I asked about Kenny, but someone told me he'd heard that Kenny had split for Hawaii. Moses had always been good for getting my anxiety up.

Before long it was time to meet Dorwina. I was proud of myself because I hadn't talked to a single woman and I'd had a good exposure. We met and were walking towards the car when I spotted a homeless guy sitting on the ground drinking coffee. I made sure that Dorwina and the other two guys were watching when I asked the man if I could have a drink of his coffee and he happily obliged. OK, I was showing off. I smiled at Dorwina as I took a sip, eating up the moment. I wasn't ready for the one-two punch she delivered.

'Hey, that guy looks like he's tripping, doesn't he, James?'

Wow. I felt myself panic. The cat was out of the bag! Dorwina knew my OCD. My first instinct was to say to her, 'Tripping on what?' I had to get a hold of myself fast! Po' White and his big buddy were smiling, waiting for me to crack. Dorwina looked over at them as if they were all in it together. What could I do or say? Of course, even if I told the staff back at the house about this, they would just say I was paranoid.

I felt like I was back in one of my old auditions, where I got so nervous I couldn't move my lips. But this wasn't stage fright – it was so far beyond that. There was no definition of this type of anxiety in good old Webster's.

I remember reading somewhere of the fight or flight theory. Whatever the hell that was, I knew it applied to me right now. It was similar to when you see one of those great actors and the moment is so real to them it's almost like they've crossed into another dimension. Sometimes they don't come back. I was there.

Suddenly the sun popped out of nowhere. Was it God? I felt its warmth spreading through me, the sun again coming to my rescue. I became calm, and remembered something Tonya had said: 'You will have these same types of people back home who knew you had problems and will try to set you off. This is good practice for you. Hang in there, and the anxiety will leave.'

With a sudden burst of courage I grabbed the cup from the old man and took another drink. I looked at the three of them; they were now wearing befuddled expressions. I held the cup up and crowed, 'Hey, this is good coffee. Would y'all like some?'

Of course, they all shook their heads.

'I wouldn't drink after anybody like that, James, if I were you,' said Dorwina.

'Hey, I got to do what I got to do!'

'Then good work, James,' said Dorwina.

I was thinking about what had happened as we made our way back to the van. You know the expression: the 'defining moment'? Well, I'd certainly had one.

I raised my fist in triumph!

THE TOKE

I was in a good mood that night as I wrote to all my email friends. I had a lot of confidence from the day's outing. I was going to take it easy and read my new *High Times* magazine that I'd bought that day to take down to Telegraph in the morning.

Just as I opened the first page, I heard somebody yelling that I had a phone call. I couldn't imagine who it was at this late hour. To my surprise it was Ray Ray. It seemed the guy she had moved in with and who'd given her a job was threatening to kill her for trying to leave him. She wanted me to come and rescue her.

'Every man wants to protect every woman from everybody but himself': those words I'd said to her turned out to be true. I told her to call the cops, but she panicked and hung up. I wanted to help Ray Ray but I couldn't think of what to do for her.

Next morning I was anxious to get to Telegraph Avenue and be by myself again. I got there and did my usual, but stayed out of the academic bookstore again because the girl from Osaka had reminded me I was making myself out to be a liar and a fool. I wandered up and down the street and eventually bumped into Jazz and Rage. I bought them two sodas and we got talking. I was caught way off guard when they told me that Squiggles was looking for me. Wow, what would Squiggles want with me? I didn't even think he knew my name and now he wanted me! What was I to do?

I asked Jazz what he wanted me for but he didn't know. I started to get anxious and thought that maybe I should get the bus back to the doughnut shop and just hang out there a while until my exposure time was up. As I turned to head for the bus, I felt a tap on my shoulder. It was Squiggles.

'Going somewhere, Jimbo?'

'Well, I have to go meet this girl. Uh, she promised me a free lunch.'

'Well, you're going to have to cancel that today because word on the street is you're a nark!'

Oh no! The words I feared the most. He grabbed my *High Times* magazine and said he heard I carried it around to get people to think I was a doper and open to buying something. Man, I was in a big jam. Squiggles had told me he'd spent time in prison before. I'd thought maybe that was all bullshit, but now it hit me that it might be true. Rabbit was standing right next to him with the ominous green briefcase.

'People tell me you talk about drugs a lot, but no one has ever got high with you. Why is that, Jimbo?' said Squiggles.

He was right. Because of my exposure I was always talking about drugs. That's the only reason I had the *High Times*, to bring up drug conversations. What could I say? I was a patient at Triumph and had a phobia about drugs? Yeah, I might as well say I was Superman.

'Well, dude, I got some 'erb, so if you're not a nark, you won't mind getting high with us, will you? So let's take a little walk down under the bridge and get oh soooooooooo high!'

I think I went into shock at that moment. I looked around at Jazz and Rage for help, but they offered nothing. After all, I'd never got high with them either so maybe they had some doubts too. Besides, Squiggles ran the area, and Jazz and Rage could say nothing even if they wanted to.

I started breathing heavily, as if I was about to have an anxiety attack. I felt maybe I was strong enough now to smoke a joint without freaking out, but I certainly wasn't sure. Just then I heard a yell.

'James, James!' I looked over and it was Ray Ray. She was standing in front of the news-stand next to a security guard.

Here was my escape. I looked at Squiggles and he motioned that it was my call. I could bail out now and take the easy way out. On the other hand this would be the ultimate exposure! It was my choice. I nodded at Ray Ray that I would see her later, as my decision was made. I walked along with Squiggles, trying to be as calm as possible. I had to keep telling myself to hang in there. If Squiggles noticed I was having an anxiety attack, he would figure I was afraid because I was a nark.

We finally got down under the bridge. Squiggles lit the joint and handed it to Jazz. Everything seemed to be happening in slow motion. All eyes were on me as they passed the joint around until it was my turn. As I slowly opened my hand . . .

'Hey, Bob, did I call my bank today?'

A loud voice suddenly came booming down from on top of the bridge. I looked up and Ralph was standing on the bridge in a three-piece suit.

'It's the heat. Everybody run for it!' I yelled out.

The punks threw the joint to the ground and scattered. Within moments everybody had disappeared. I quickly gathered myself and walked up to Ralph, still standing on the bridge, and hugged him.

'Where in the hell did you come from? And where did you get that suit?'

'This is a suit bankers wear. I am wearing it to desensitise myself about my finances. Do I look gay in it? Is that why you hugged me? If so, I'll take it back.'

'No, Ralph, you're obsessing! You look real professional. Like a banker.'

Ralph smiled from ear to ear. A moment later we crossed the street to where Ralph had parked his car and drove off. Ralph had just saved me. Would I have smoked that joint?

One thing was certain: I would never laugh at Ralph again.

MARCHING ORDERS

I was feeling good the next day. I had just had a meeting with Jimmy, my social worker, and he had given me encouragement about staying for four months. I had been here now for about two and a half and wasn't ready to leave. I gave him the old line, 'I want to volunteer to help the homeless first to see how I react around people for more than just an hour.' He was all for it, and was calling some shelters around Telegraph Avenue. Who knows, I was thinking, I might meet some nice Asian girl working there, too.

Everything was going fine until curfew. I headed up the stairs and spotted Mary trying to get Linzy away from the radio. Meanwhile Ralph kept asking Mary if he could call his banker, and some guy I didn't know was counting his steps as he walked back and forth in front of her. It was hilarious, all three going at her at once:

'I have to check my finances or I can't sleep,' yelled Ralph.

'Go to bed right now, Ralph,' said Mary.

'If you don't let me call the bank, I'll get my dad to buy this place and everybody in it. Except Bob.'

I couldn't help myself. I burst out laughing on the stairway. It was surreal watching Mary trying to deal with this as the counter continued to count his steps right in front of her.

'James, get to bed now!' she said.

Now, I did something I would regret for a long time. The reasons are complicated. On some level I knew it would be the last straw. But I did it anyway. I said, 'I can't, I'm in the middle of a ritual.'

I continued to laugh until she finally got me to go to my room. I knew I had promised not to laugh at Ralph, but my resolve had only lasted a day. I just couldn't help myself.

Next morning I forgot all about it and headed for the Park. Jazz and everyone were completely fine with me and Jazz even told me that Squiggles wanted to thank me when he got back from making a deal. Wow! I was feeling great as I did my usual routine and then headed home for lunch.

I got in the lunch queue as soon as I reached the house and a moment later one of the male counsellors intercepted me and told me that Tonya wanted to see me in the TV room. No big deal. Maybe she wanted to change our meeting time.

I walked in and opened the door. To my dismay, Jimmy, Tonya and the big cheese, Miss Hines, were all sitting at a table. I knew I was in trouble.

Tonya spoke first. 'James, laughing at patients and interfering with counsellors won't be tolerated.'

I started to say something when Tonya spoke the words of doom: 'You will have to be out by the end of the week.'

My world came crashing down on me.

'Please don't kick me out! I won't ever do it again!'

I started crying and begging and pleading. No good. Tonya said the decision had already been made. I tried to argue with her that she should at least hear my side of the story before going ahead with a decision of that magnitude. I tried it on Jimmy, but he said I had already been warned the first time I'd met with him and the Doc.

Where was the Doc? He was the only one that could save me. He was in New York and wouldn't be back until Thursday. I even tried to get an extra week, saying I couldn't afford a plane ticket unless I made a two weeks' advanced purchase. But Miss Hines said the date was final and that they would have another patient coming to take my place.

'I've sabotaged myself again. I always do and I always will!' I said to anybody who might have listened. I got no response. One of Tonya's phrases suddenly came back to me, and I quickly tried to use it on her. 'I wasn't laughing at my fellow patients or the counsellor. I was laughing at the situation,' I said.

Tonya looked the other way.

A moment later I stumbled out of the door, still in shock.

What was I to do? I didn't want to go home. I decided I had to get a hold of myself quickly and get into my manipulating mode. I would do whatever was necessary.

I ran to the computer and emailed the Doc, who was good about checking his messages. I told him the situation. I got a message back saying he couldn't overrule the staff: that would be bad for morale. Whatever happened to that 'you'll never get kicked out' line he had given me? I emailed him right back and asked if he would at least talk to Miss Hines. He said he would.

I ran over to her office and told her the Doc wanted to talk to her about the matter. She said that she would, but that I shouldn't get my hopes up. Of course, I didn't tell her about the first email he'd sent me. I had to sit down and figure out what my options were. I was supposed to meet with Tonya tomorrow at our regular meeting time, but there was no way I was going to show up there. I felt she had betrayed me. She was cold, like Amos said. Of course, my making jokes about her height didn't help either.

Who would be on my side, I wondered. How about Jimmy? No, he hadn't said a word in my defence. Miss Hines wasn't an option. I remembered other patients who had been asked to leave, but they were all told they could come back in six months' time. Not me. I had committed the cardinal sin: I'd laughed at fellow patients. Hell, when you get well, all this stuff seems ridiculous. I even laughed at myself for all the crazy stuff I had done before coming here.

I could talk to Ralph and get him to talk to Miss Hines. Yeah, get Linzy too. I ran up to their rooms.

'You got kicked out of where?' said Linzy.

'I will talk to my banker about it,' said Ralph.

If my fate depended on these two, I was history.

I saw Mary, and went over and laid a guilt trip on her.

'Mary, I got kicked out because of the notes you wrote about me last night. It might help if you told Miss Hines I was really having an anxiety attack and couldn't move when you told me to get upstairs.'

Mary told me she was terribly sorry and walked away. She was a sweet girl, and I figured she would go and ask Miss Hines to reconsider.

OK, things were in motion. Maybe I could beat this. To be honest I was afraid I couldn't cut it on the outside. Sure, I was confident at Telegraph and even at the Park. But I always knew I was coming home to my safety net: Within Reach. I was so desperate I would do anything to stay!

I walked into the kitchen for dinner and was about to tell Barney the bad news when Po' White walked over.

'Have a nice trip home, James!'

'You little bastard! You want to go outside?'

A counsellor happened to be standing right there. She told me to cool down and go outside. I tried to argue with her, but to no avail. I decided right then that if I had to go, I would have company. Another idea came to me. I remembered other patients requesting a couple of extra days – the weekend, for example. Not only would it give me a couple more days to manipulate whomever I could, but I could also get a cheaper air fare if worst came to worst.

I walked into Miss Hines's office, but she was gone for the day and her assistant was there. I asked the assistant if I could stay on Saturday and Sunday. She wasn't aware of my circumstances and said she thought it would be OK. Now I got some confidence back. A little.

I was in a fantasy land, like Amos had said. Of course, I didn't want to leave. Group that night was quiet because Barney was sad about my being kicked out. My scores for the day were real for the first time since I'd arrived. My day was a zero and my anxiety was a ten. Even though I had got much better, it really bothered me that I was being expelled. I had a queasy feeling all night.

I went to the Park the next morning and stayed completely in character. I told Jazz and the gang that I was hitchhiking to New Orleans at the end of the week.

'That is one dangerous town. Why in the fuck are you going there?' asked Jazz.

I really didn't have an answer for that.

I walked over to get my daily Dr Pepper and felt very sad. I had been terrified of druggies for years and now two of my best friends were Jazz and Rage: two drug addicts! I would miss them.

I told them I had found a wallet with forty dollars in it and that lunch was my treat. They excitedly agreed. It was an ironic friendship for sure. Time was getting on, so I figured no mess-ups: go catch the bus on time and go straight back for the next group. As I was leaving, I saw Squiggles selling drugs to more kids. He waved to me as if I were cool now and not a nark. I couldn't worry about him now. I had my own problems.

I made my way down the Avenue and stood at the bus stop. A moment later this beautiful blonde girl came up and asked me where UC Berkeley was. She had an accent. I asked her if it was German and she said no, Swedish. Wow! She looked like one of those bikini-clad Swedish girls on the adverts, playing beach volleyball or drinking beer or whatever the hell they'd be doing. I looked at my watch and knew I had to catch my bus.

Before I knew it I was walking her towards the campus and inviting her for coffee. To this day, no matter what kind of line I feed these women, I'm still amazed why they would even consider having coffee with me.

Before I knew it, a half-hour had passed. I had to get going, but there was no way I could make it onto the bus in time. I got the nice Swedish girl's email address and took off running down the street, looking for a cab. I told the driver if I didn't get to Triumph in ten minutes I would lose my job.

'Well, it's a fifteen-minute drive,' he said.

I laid an extra twenty on him.

'Now it's an eight-minute drive.'

I made it just in time for roll call. After the meeting I went over to check my email. I was hoping Dr Swenson would somehow come to my rescue. I spotted Linzy staring at the radio again.

'James, I got great news for you. I talked to Miss Hines!'

'Great, Linzy! What's the good news?'

'I told her you keep bugging me about the radio so I have decided to leave this place. So now you won't be alone. I will be leaving on Friday with you!'

I was devastated. Linzy was beaming from ear to ear. The hole I'd dug myself was getting deeper and deeper. I must have been out of my mind to send Linzy in there to talk to her. Linzy was just like a little child.

'Hey, James, I only did that because my parents are spending all my inheritance money on this place. I want that money just for me!' said Linzy.

Realistically the hospital would lose around thirty grand if she left, and that didn't reflect well on me.

A few minutes later the girl I had talked to about staying through the weekend came in and angrily said I would have to be out by Friday. Man, I was in deep. Dr Swenson was my only hope and he would be in on Thursday. It also hit me in my panic mode that still no one had mentioned anything about my coming back. Desperate people do desperate things. I would have to go and see Miss Hines and give it a shot.

As I walked towards her office, I heard a familiar voice. It was Po' White.

'Yes, everybody is so much happier now that James is leaving. Everybody was walking on pins and needles around here. I mean, you never knew when he might go off!'

A moment later I heard Miss Hines say, 'Don't worry, he'll be out of here by Friday.'

I think at that moment reality set in. I was history. I was now more determined than ever to carry through on my promise to myself: if I was leaving, that son of a bitch Po' White Trash was coming with me.

But, in the big picture, Squiggles was more important.

THE BIG PICTURE

I tried to keep a low profile. Thursday finally came and the Doc was back. I bought a plane ticket with seven days' notice, so if worst came to worst and I really was leaving, I somehow had to get the last weekend in here. When I told my dear old dad I was coming home and needed the airfare, he suggested I catch the bus again. That way I could see the country. The man was so obsessed with money that it made me sick.

I told my dad, 'Hey, you never asked me if I got any better!'

His response was, 'Oh yeah, are you the same?'

What a guy.

Linzy came up to me on the computer and said, 'Aren't you excited about us leaving together, James?'

I looked angrily at her but she looked so out of it I couldn't help but feel sorry for her. 'Sure,' I said.

A short time later Tonya came looking for me and told me

I had missed our meeting and that I was supposed to make sure I was at the next one tomorrow morning. Yeah, right! I had nothing to say to her.

I walked into Dr Swenson's office for my last appointment, and before I could say anything he admonished me.

'I see you got yourself kicked out!'

This final stake pierced my heart! It was over.

I finally spoke up. 'Could I stay until Monday? My plane won't leave until then.'

'No, Jimmy and Tonya think it's better you leave Friday. You're having a negative influence on Linzy.'

The world collapsed in front of my eyes. 'You bastards throw me out in the street like garbage! You don't give a shit about me! I'm nothing to you. And yeah, what about all that bullshit: hey, you'll never get kicked out. What crap that was!'

The Doctor looked at me like never before.

'OK, you're pissed. You knew on Monday that you had to be out by Friday. You want to leave this place pissed, that's your choice. On the other hand you told me at the last session that you have gotten so much better here that it was almost unbelievable. "The big picture": remember that?'

He was right. I was feeling sorry for myself and wasn't looking at the big picture.

'Yeah, Doc. The big picture is that I'm ninety per cent better! I can laugh again. I can have lunch with people. I can do any fricking thing I want!'

Tears ran down my face as the last 20 years flashed before me. So maybe I wasn't a good person. But no one – and I mean no one – deserves to suffer like I did. Yes, I had been given another chance in life. Maybe I could see the movie a second time now.

'Hey, Doc, I'm going to kick your ass in basketball tonight!'

'Bring it on, big boy!'

The Doc reiterated that I had to keep pushing the envelope or I would have a relapse. I had to get structure and have an after-care programme.

'Hey, Doc, it still bothers me that I got kicked out. I mean, it leaves a bad taste in my mouth.'

'Well, like you said, see the big picture and that's what's important.'

I pondered a moment and spoke the truth. 'There are consequences for everything we do in life, huh, Doc?'

The Doc just smiled at me and I think he was proud that I'd owned up to it.

I walked out of the door happy. Of course, I did leave the door open a little. I said something about, 'If I ever need to come back . . .' and the Doc said that that would be possible.

I shocked everybody at group that night when I said my day was a ten and my anxiety was a zero. Of course, Barney wanted to know why, so I told him I was at least ninety per cent better. Everybody looked at me strangely. Of course, there was a lot of jealousy, too: human nature. I even gave everybody positive feedback and told them they had to take risks to get better.

Things got even better at basketball when the Doc asked one of his ex-patients if I could stay over at his place for the weekend. The guy was honoured the Doc had even asked. I never really realised how Dr Swenson had this aura, because he was always making jokes and making light of things. But he had something. All the ex-patients lived for this basketball game once a week. The sun was always shining when you were around him. Because of him, my life had changed forever.

LAST DAY

The last day was very strange. I decided to stay away from Telegraph and the Park. I'm sure Dorwina was happy I was going, but she kept a low profile with me, and actually came up and wished me good luck. I knew she didn't mean it. I figured she was a bit scared of me. I mean, I wasn't in the psycho ward but we all had emotional problems and could be dangerous. I came to the conclusion that she knew I had nothing to lose because I was leaving, so she'd better tread softly with me.

Mary was a sweet girl and I would miss her.

I got on the Internet and wrote the Doc an email. It went like this:

> I feel sad today. I know I will never see you and Alley and the guys from basketball again. I want you to know I've never had any friends before, but you are my friends. I'm crying again. Isn't that funny? I never cried for 20 years and now I turn into a big baby. It's hard for me to say what I want to say to y'all with all these emotions running around in my head. I wrote a poem for you and the guys and it goes something like this:
>
> As I walk around the park this gloomy day, I feel sadness as my friends are going away.
>
> The leaves change colours, the ducks fly south, nightfall turns into morning. Things are always evolving and never remain the same.
>
> Suddenly the sun bursts out and I feel warmth! Yes, it comes to me now that it doesn't matter about time, distance, or place. You are my friends!

Mary happened to walk by and noticed I was in tears. I showed her my letter. I wanted her to know that I wasn't holding her responsible for my expulsion. She comforted me as I wailed like a baby. Tonya came over and tried to console me and I said to her, 'Please leave me alone! Mary is helping me get through this.'

She walked away. Would I change my mind about Tonya after I left here and reflected?

I pulled myself together and sent the email.

I heard Po' White Trash laughing in the other room. I had work to do.

THE PLAN

I got my thoughts together and came up with the perfect plan for Po' White. I had got his email address from the big guy. I'd told him I wanted to send everyone a goodbye letter. Naivety – oh, what a beautiful quality. I had also got myself an email address from Yahoo under the name of 'Mary from Triumph'.

Here was my plan: I emailed Po' White as Mary and said, 'I know this is totally against the rules and I'm risking my whole career but I can't stop thinking about you. I want you in the worst way and have to have you! So please come to my office at 7 a.m. One more thing, I want you totally naked when you enter my office! PS: Don't worry, we won't get caught, because no one comes in before 8.'

I sent the email and I knew he would take the bait. Alley surprised me while I was on the Net.

'You saying your goodbyes to your Asian babes?'

Oh, Alley. She had that great smile! I would miss her terribly, but I didn't want to get choked up with her too. I had never seen her show any emotion in all the groups. I had a feeling there were a tonne of tears buried deep inside her, but perhaps they would lie dormant forever. She had stayed away from me since I'd made that crack about having a thing for her. She was a special girl.

We hugged awkwardly. I felt myself getting choked up again. I knew that would bother her, so I fought it as hard as I could and made a joke to try to lighten things up.

Thank God Barney came up and started his usual rambling.

'Oh, James: saved everybody but couldn't save himself!'

I told him he owed me one and that I wanted him to take out Po' White at the next basketball game. Po' White didn't show up for last night's game and had good reason not to.

'Hey, James, say pooo' white trash. I love the way you say it!' said Barney. 'Pooooooooooooooooooooooo' white trash!' I said.

'Hey, we'll ask Alley to guard Po' White. Everybody is afraid of her out there,' said Barney.

I had to laugh as Alley walked away. I still wanted to know where she disappeared to all those days and nights. She always seemed to get back right before curfew. Oh, what the hell. Give the girl a break.

'James, one more poooo' white. It drives me crazy!' said Barney.

We both said it together: 'Pooooooooooooooooo' white trash!'

'You kill me, James.'

Barney proceeded to tell me that Anna and the Christian hooked up in his room the past night. I was surprised, because Anna had this very handsome boyfriend who visited her all the time. He also must have been a great guy to put up with her OCD. As for the Christian, I wasn't surprised. Practising celibacy for a woman is one thing. Man is a different animal altogether. A woman has no idea whatsoever how strong the sexual drive is in a man. It's indescribable. Women's libbers wouldn't exist if they had the chance to be a man for just one day.

Anna was a sweet girl so I assumed that she and the Christian could share things her boyfriend couldn't comprehend.

Barney told me he had bought a cake for my going-away party that night. That was nice of him. Barney had something most of us didn't have: money. Most of us were dependent on Medicare and disability cheques from the government, but Barney's dad would take care of him forever. Then again, that might be his downfall. He had an out and we didn't. Maybe that made us more desperate to get better.

The party was just about as expected. They had a card that everybody signed except Po' White Trash. In truth the only patients I would miss were Alley and Barney. After the party I started getting my stuff together. I started thinking about Po' White Trash. Of course, I hated the guy, but maybe I was going too far. I decided that after I washed my clothes, I would tell him the email was just a going-away gag. I made my way down to the washer and dryer. To my surprise both were full of clothes. We had a schedule, and I was the only one on it. I got pissed and dragged all the clothes out and threw them onto the counter. A few moments later guess who showed up? Po' White and the big guy.

'What are our clothes doing on the counter? Who gave you permission to take them out?' said Po' White Trash.

My blood started to boil. The son of a bitch hadn't washed his clothes for two months, but now, on the night

I was leaving, he did. Shit, the bastard didn't even have clothes when he came. I was just about to grab him around the throat when one of the counsellors came walking by.

'James took our clothes out of the dryer and they weren't even dry!' said Po' White.

I told the counsellor that it was true, but that I was the only one scheduled to wash that night. He told them that I was right and they could only use it after I was done. I smiled as he walked away.

I thought that was the end of it and started to go upstairs, but Po' White and the big guy didn't budge. Now I was thinking, if I go upstairs, they're going to stop the washer or throw dirt on my clothes. Paranoid? Maybe. The problem was the dryer didn't work right and took hours to do its job. Shit, I had other things to do.

'Listen, if either one of you two bastards touches my clothes, I will . . .'

Just then Miss Hines's assistant came out of nowhere.

'That's why you're being kicked out, James. Talking to fellow patients that way.'

I tried to explain the circumstances but she wasn't listening. She was still pissed that I'd got permission from her to stay over the weekend and Miss Hines had jumped all over her about that, I'm sure.

I sat down for a moment and tried to gather myself. I wanted to tell this woman off big time but that would ruin any chance of me ever coming back. I had to bite the bullet. Po' White, though, was a different story.

MY EXIT

I couldn't sleep much, and woke up at 5.45 a.m. I was going to take a cab to the Doc's friend's house to stay for the weekend. I was leaving at 7 a.m. I didn't want to say goodbye again to anybody. It was just too heart wrenching. I also wanted to see what would happen with Po' White. Maybe he was smarter than I thought and would back out.

I heard the cab honking for me just before seven, so I made my way down the stairs. I guess I would never know Po' White's fate. I hoped he would remember to take his toothbrush with him on his way out. Then again, I don't think he had one!

SQUIGGLES: EXIT STAGE LEFT

Now that my business with Po' White was over, I had to complete my mission: Squiggles. Still, I had to laugh thinking about Po' White Trash. He was the skinniest, most unwholesome-looking person I had ever seen. If things went my way, poor Mary.

Down to business. The guy I was staying with had so many OCD problems that he steered clear of me. That was good; I had to have a plan. I had to get my hands on that green briefcase. That was the key to Squiggles's demise. Jazz had mentioned during one of his drunken sprees that Squiggles was just a small frog in the drug pond; that it wasn't his money or drugs, but he got a commission on his sales. I realised that if I got rid of the briefcase, Squiggles would be in big trouble.

I waited until Saturday night. I ended up wandering

around Telegraph Avenue until I ran into Jazz standing with Rabbit. Squiggles, they said, had gone over to the pizza parlour. I told them I had met this guy with a lot of bread who told me he was looking for a connection to score a lot of speed and would give me a hundred dollars' travel money if I hooked him up. Where had this plan come from? It had just hit me at that moment.

Jazz quickly went after Squiggles, hoping he would be compensated. I started getting nervous. I was way over my head and I didn't really know what I was going to do. I was always good at improv in my old acting classes. The thought suddenly hit me that only one guy was holding the briefcase. I caught myself staring at it. Maybe it was the idea that I had been so terrified of drugs for the last 15 years and, lo and behold, every illegal drug known to mankind was sitting right next to me! I had to do something and do it quickly.

Ahhh – an explosion suddenly went off in my head. What was the sole objective of every druggie out here?

'Hey, Rabbit, why don't we share some 'erb before Squiggles and Jazz get back?'

'Why, you got some?' said Rabbit.

'No, but I'm sure you do, and when I finish this deal with Squiggles, I'll have plenty of bread to keep you high for weeks!'

'We can't smoke out here on Telegraph, dude,' said Rabbit.

My plan was working. All I had to do was get rid of this spaced-out zombie for a minute.

'OK, dude, you go into the alley and take a couple of tokes. When you get back, I will,' I said.

He agreed, but grabbed the briefcase to take it with him.

'Hey, dude, leave the case out here. I got travel money riding on this deal, and if something happened to you, well, we're both fucked!'

He hesitated, so I quickly added, 'Hey, remember, dude, I'm the one who tipped everybody off the other day when that cop showed up.'

He pondered a moment before saying, 'I got orders never to leave the bag.'

He slowly drifted behind the coffee shop and out of sight. Damn it! I started to get real nervous. Squiggles would be here any moment. I had to do something quickly. I looked around a moment then careered off into the alley. Rabbit had the case over his shoulder as he smoked a joint. I had to get the bag and make a run for it. I knew if I got it in my hands, no one would catch me. I had been jogging for years with 15-lb weights. I used to throw them up and catch them as I ran. Yes, it was some form of OCD. I remember people used to come up to me and say, 'Hey, you're the weird guy who runs with weights!'

This day my weirdness would pay off. I hesitated a moment. I would have all those drugs in my hands. I quickly focused my thoughts on the young boys that Squiggles was hustling drugs to.

I turned and kicked Rabbit in the knee as hard as I could! He moaned and momentarily lost his balance. I jerked the case from his shoulder and flew out of the alley. I ran like hell! I was shaking like a leaf, not because of Rabbit and Squiggles, but because I had all those drugs in my hands. Yes, I was cured, but not a hundred per cent. To make things worse it started to rain. Not a sprinkle, but a downpour.

I ran and ran and ran. My heart pounded like never before. I wanted to get far enough away to dump the case. But where? I thought about a trash can, but I knew from experience that the homeless go through them every morning for their breakfast. I spotted a café with a big dumpster. That was my answer. I looked around to see if anybody was near me and looked into it to see how full it was. All that was in it was a big puddle of rainwater. I threw the briefcase in, hearing the splash as it hit the bottom.

Now what? Where could I go? What other place gave me peace besides Within Reach and Telegraph Avenue? The good old doughnut shop. Not only would I be safe there, but I also had fond memories of Yuki and others who had showed me kindness.

GOODBYE ALLEY

The rain began to let up. I figured I had run about a mile away from Telegraph so I wouldn't be spotted waiting on a bus. One pulled up soon enough and I made it to the shop. It was open 24 hours so I thought about staying there until that morning and then catching a cab to the airport. But I remembered my luggage was at the Doc's friend's. I knew I couldn't sleep. All that adrenalin was still pumping.

I was pondering all that had happened when the 'mystery woman' popped in the doughnut shop.

'Well, I never thought I would see you again, James.'

Wow. I felt very peaceful now. I guess I could add Alley to my list of calming influences.

'You look rough, James. Tough night at Telegraph Avenue?'

'You have no idea, my friend.'

I thought about telling her what had happened but then thought better of it.

'Well, I've got my curfew, James. I just came to get some coffee to go.'

She paused at the door, searching for something to say. 'I'm sorry, James, for avoiding you after you said you had feelings for me . . . I have many issues and I'm afraid to get close to anyone.'

I understood her statement more than anybody in the whole world. Who knows, maybe in another life we could have hopped that freight together and rode forever and ever! But that wasn't to be.

'Don't worry about it, Alley, I understand all too clearly.'

Alley nervously smiled and grabbed the door.

'One more thing before you leave . . . please tell me where you go all the time. It's been killing me wondering.'

'Oh, what the hell. Trust me: it's weird.'

'I'm listening.'

'I go down to the Aids hospice where seriously sick children are treated. I want to give blood so bad but my OCD fear of contamination stops me. I just stand and stare at the babies, hoping one night I will have the courage to walk in and give blood. I've been going there every night, but I always chicken out. I'm thinking one special night I'll give in and do it. I mean, if sick children can't motivate you, what can? Right, James?'

I wanted to have an answer for her, but I didn't. I wasn't surprised by what she told me. She was one in a million.

Now it was time to say goodbye to Alley. I knew I would never see her again.

'I'm gone in the morning and back to reality.'

'Are you scared, James?'

'Yeah. Terrified!'

'You'll make it, James.'

'Why do you say that?'

'You're different from the rest of us.'

'How so?'

'I can't explain it, but you are. It's like your inner demons propel you to be more determined.'

I nodded, said goodbye and quickly walked away to the restroom. I still hated goodbyes. I was crying now. I waited to regain my composure and went outside.

I started making my way over to the bus stop when I heard Alley's familiar voice coming from up the street. 'Hey, James!'

'Yeah?' I said.

'You've been loved!'

THE CAB RIDE

The cab came to pick me up from the Doc's friend's house in the morning. I tried to remember how I was feeling on my first ride into Berkeley. I started thinking about Amos and the girl from Texas. I knew now how scared they were. We were in the real world now. No safety nets. I wanted the ride to last forever. I even kept thinking that maybe the cabbie would get a flat, prolonging my journey back to reality.

I tried telling myself that even if I were able to stay the last two weeks or even an extra month, I still would have come to this point. It was inevitable. I would be sitting in a cab, alone and scared. It had been one hell of a ride these last two and a half months. The people I'd met – it seemed almost surreal: like I had been watching a long movie and was waiting for it to end.

The cab driver snapped me back to the present when he opened the door for me and asked for the fare. The rest was a haze and before I knew it, I was on the plane waiting for it to take off.

I looked out of the window and the sun was shining. If I

had beaten this, I could defeat my impulse to chat up women. Yes! I could conquer it!

I felt someone grab me. I turned around and this beautiful Asian woman asked me if I was OK. I nodded. She turned away. I looked out of the window again, trying to regain my composure.

A moment later I turned back and said, 'I bet you're from Japan, aren't you?'

What the hell, one out of two ain't bad!

MAN, INTERRUPTED

A few years have passed since I left Triumph. I started off doing great. I continued to push the envelope: touching trash cans and shaking hands, etc.

That wouldn't last, however.

Maybe I got too confident because, two years later, I quit taking my medication and did no exposure therapy. Then an incident happened and I snapped and wanted to go back to Triumph. The Doc turned out to be right when he said a relapse was inevitable if I didn't have an after-care programme.

Funny, they didn't want me to come back. The powers that be said no thanks.

I guess there are two ways of looking at that. One – and this is my personal belief – is that after two years these good-hearted liberal people should have given me, or anyone, for that matter, another chance. Or two – which is their point of view – why put up with this manipulating bully, etc. etc. etc. one more time?

You make the call.

That said, the good Doc ended up coming through as he

wasn't even aware they'd rejected my application and said I could come back on a trial basis. A short time later my meds kicked in and I started doing my own exposures again. I managed to get back to a point where I didn't need a return visit after all.

Lately I've been doing really well, and have my symptoms in check – more or less. Of course, there are occasional relapses. I continue to do my exposures, going up to street people, shaking hands and sharing food, and things of that nature. Of course, I always have this fear that one day I will wake up and be sick again. I couldn't go back to that!

I decided to write this book mostly to keep my mind busy. I had been bragging to everyone at Within Reach that I was going to do it and it dawned on me that it could be a fascinating book – and I might even help somebody along the way.

I've also come to realise how wrong I was about everyone at Within Reach. If it wasn't for that institution, I would probably be dead now. I've been given a second chance in life, and it's all because of the doctors and counsellors at the clinic.

I have to admit, I am a controversial guy. If a strange man came up and handed me a one-hundred-dollar bill, I would be pissed that he hadn't given me five twenties. That's the kind of guy I am. As for the woman impulse thing, it's getting a little better. It's slowly hitting me that some young girl really would have no interest in me! I've tried to wean myself off it by making a rule only to talk to Asian women. My theory is that in the small town I live in, there might be only two or three. Hey, I'm trying.

The thing that haunts me more than anything is what would have happened if they had kicked me out a month earlier. Would I still be around, writing this book? I email the Doc all the time about that. That will haunt me forever.

This book would not have been possible without the following people: Dr David Rees in Lafayette, Louisiana, who kept hanging in there with me and gave me my first glimpse that I wasn't schizophrenic; Mel Brooks, who has taken my phone calls for 20 years and inspired me to write even as I lived out of my car and wrote in laundromats to stay warm; Mary and all the counsellors, who put up with my misguided anger; my brother, who has helped me; Jen Knapper, a sweet Christian girl who emailed me consistently during one of my darkest periods, pleading with me not to commit suicide – to this day, she is in New Guinea, spreading her faith; my friend Ron in Lake Charles – you know who you are; Yahoo Briefcase, which gave me restful nights because I knew I had my material saved; all the nice Asian girls in Berkeley who took the time to share a moment with me; and, of course, all the street people from People's Park and Telegraph Avenue, and my fellow patients, who populate the pages of this book.

I remember a couple of years ago when I first wrote the book an agent told me that some people would appreciate the book and some wouldn't. I am extremely happy that my publisher Bill Campbell had the vision to take it on. Many thanks also to Kevin O'Brien, who did a marvellous job of editing it. Thanks also to all the staff at Mainstream Publishing, who helped to make my dream a reality.

Special thanks go to my manager, Patrick Hughes, who shared my enthusiasm from the beginning.

And on a sad note, I dedicate this book to my mother. I told her I was sorry for the way I'd treated her, even though I still had anger towards her and hardly ever visited her in the rest home she was at. A year later she passed away. I'd thought that when she died I would be free of my insecurities toward women, that all my mistrust would somehow disappear. I found out quickly that this was not to be.

My father contracted throat cancer and ended up losing his voice. Since then he has tried to help me, always making sure I have a vehicle to drive and money to get my medication.

I've got to run now; I hear a train whistling in the distance, and there are many, many moments left to seek!